I Learned It through the Grapevine

I Learned It through the Grapevine

Wisdom Comes in Bunches

Todd Soltysiak

I LEARNED IT THROUGH THE GRAPEVINE
Copyright © 2019 by Todd Soltysiak

Scriptures taken from the Holy Bible, New International Version®, NIV®. Copyright © 1973, 1978, 1984, 2011 by Biblica, Inc.™ Used by permission of Zondervan. All rights reserved worldwide. www.zondervan.com The "NIV" and "New International Version" are trademarks registered in the United States Patent and Trademark Office by Biblica, Inc.™

Print ISBN: 978-1-4866-1870-5
eBook ISBN: 978-1-4866-1871-2

Word Alive Press
119 De Baets Street Winnipeg, MB R2J 3R9
www.wordalivepress.ca

WORD ALIVE
—PRESS—

Cataloguing in Publication information can be obtained from Library and Archives Canada.

To the earthly love of my life,
Sheila Ann,
You have made each day worth living.
I will love you forever and then some!

To the heavenly love of my life,
Jesus,
Thank you for never giving up on me or forgetting me.
This book is for you.

Contents

Acknowledgements

This book wouldn't have been possible without a "great cloud of witnesses," and I'm forever in your debt. To my advance readers—Sarah, Bruce, Mark, Annette, Betsy, Paul, Klaus, Kat, and of course Poppa—thank you for encouraging me. I sat on pins and needles wondering why you hadn't finished it yet! But thank you for taking the time. Your friendship means the world to me.

To Terry Atkinson (Dr. T), thank you for the guidance and feedback. You are my pastor, but I count you as a friend. In the short time you've been here at Heart Lake Baptist Church, you have infiltrated our lives. Thank you! Your detailed review of the manuscript was so helpful and encouraging… I can never thank you enough.

To Kat, thank you for graciously allowing me to use some of your story. You have become a part of our family, and our lives have become entwined. You've come so far and the Lord has His hand on your life. You will crush mountains someday with the faith the Lord has given you.

To Sheila, thank you for encouraging, reading, editing, re-editing, and generally talking me off the ledge a few times. Thank you for putting up with me. You're stuck with me… another fifty years!

To Mr. Zazzle, thank you for keeping me company on those cold winter days on the couch writing this book. Me typing… you snoring! You have a special talent for teaching me what it means to "abide."

Maybe there's a book there, but your ever-present desire just to be with me has made me a better person.

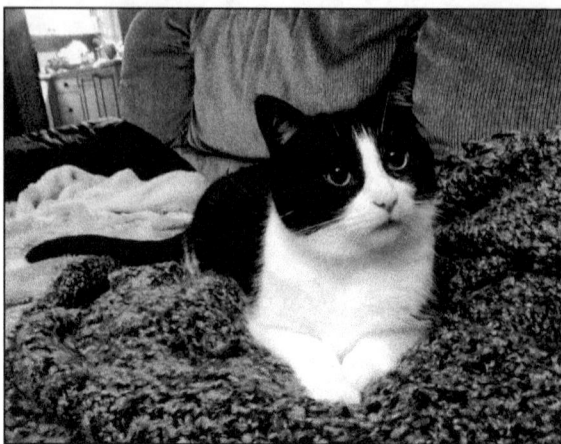

Zazzle

Introduction

Audacity is defined as the willingness to take bold risks, to have courage or confidence of a kind that people find shocking.

In a way, this book is my act of audacity. You'll notice that I don't have the designation "Doctor" in front of my name, and I'm certainly not one of the well-known mega-church leaders and writers many of you may be familiar with. I'm simply a man who has a burning love of God and my Lord Jesus Christ. A story had developed in my life that I needed to share, that I felt compelled to share.

This book has been fifteen years in the making, but it's mostly come together within the last year. The shocking thing is how quickly it came together once I overcame my fear.

Writing a book is a daunting undertaking to ponder. I've done some hiking in mountainous terrain, and my best comparison to writing a book are the thoughts and feelings that race through your head when you stand at the base of a large mountain. Sometimes you can see the summit and glimpse where you're hoping to end up. Other times you're standing in the parking lot, looking at a map that shows you the route to the top, but you have no vision of the end goal. You can't see the summit.

That's what writing this book was like for me. I had an idea of what the route would look like, but I had no idea how it was going to turn out.

The book took fifteen years to write mostly because, for fourteen and a half years, God was instructing me, pruning me, teaching me, and planting seeds of inspiration that would take a significant time to mature. I needed to be taught insights and wisdom to share this book with you. As you'll find out, some of my lessons came fast, others came painfully slow, and sometimes I wasn't the sharpest knife in the drawer.

The idea for this book started with some feedback I got from friends as I shared some of my experiences and observations while working in my vineyard. My friends are very gracious and I love them to pieces. They were there when I first planted my vineyard and they tolerated me talking about tending the vines, complaining about disease, and taking in the harvest. They never turned down a glass of wine to celebrate either!

But when I shared with them how I felt God was revealing Himself to me, and how I was learning about Him in a deep and profound way, about how He deals with us and how the world works, they encouraged me to share my experiences.

So the seed was planted.

Here's what happens when kingdom seed is planted. The enemy shows up and starts to discourage you, whisper thoughts of doubt, and basically try to kill the seed before it grows.

The writing didn't start for a long time because I delayed it.

Who do you think you are? I thought. *You're not a writer. You're not a pastor or a preacher. You have no credibility. It'll all be a waste of time.*

And to my shame, I listened to that voice for a while. But you know what? God had other plans. He is relentless. The story wouldn't leave me, and the need to write it kept coming back.

The enemy was certainly a factor in the delay, but I also think it wasn't yet the right season for the full book to come together. As you read, you'll be introduced to a registered charity called Rising Angels that my wife Sheila and I started in 2015 with our spiritual daughter, Katarina (Kat) MacLeod. Rising Angels was founded to help bring sex trade education to professionals and the public, and to provide supportive services to women exploited by the sex trade, allowing them to experience physical, mental, social, and spiritual restoration.

You see, Kat was exploited as a prostitute for fifteen years. Her story is one of survival, salvation, and restoration, and I think God needed me to meet Kat, to be a part of her story and life, to give me some of what I needed to write this book.

Over the course of reading, you'll learn more about Kat, how we met, her life, and better understand the issue of human trafficking. I hope and pray that if what you read makes you curious or angry, that it inspires you to take action and reach out to us. Hopefully you will educate yourself on this cause and get involved in the fight. We need you![1]

In the end, this book is about fruit. Fruit of the vine. Kingdom fruit. Fruit that will last. God's fruit. It's a journey of discovery. It's about our calling to bear fruit in this lost and dark generation, our calling to demonstrate the love of Christ to a world that desperately needs to hear the Good News, that needs to know that God is alive.

He is still actively tending the vineyard. He wants to make you the best fruit-bearer you can be. He wants to unleash you into the world to show and tell how massively wonderful He is.

I learned all this by toiling in my vineyard, by getting my hands dirty, and by spending time up close and personal with grapes and vines over the course of many seasons. These are hard-won lessons for me, and I can only hope and pray that they will help you to see God anew, love God anew, and inspire you to get your hands dirty for the Gospel.

To some of you, what I'm saying is old hat, and you've heard it before. That's okay. I think it's important for us to be reminded time and time again about a story that never grows old. I would ask that you stick with the journey and not gloss over anything.

I've included some provoking and challenging study questions at the end of each chapter. Sheila and I were youth leaders at our church for fifteen years, and trust me when I tell you that I've seen my fair share of lame study questions. I've tried to make these questions

---

[1] To contact us, visit www.risingangels.net.

open-ended enough that you'll be forced to wrestle with difficult topics. If you struggle, or if they cause you some discomfort, good! What you're experiencing is pruning. A large part of this book is about pruning, and dealing with pain. I hope you'll walk away having a new, or at least different, perspective on pruning.

I started off by saying that this book was fourteen years, six months in the prepping, and six months in the actual writing. Amazingly, once I actually laid out the chapters, and covered the seasons and activities of the vineyard, the book seemed to flow like water.

Sheila works as a librarian, and she goes to work on Saturdays. We have a tradition that every Saturday morning I make her breakfast before she goes to work. In the spring, summer, and fall, I'll be busy either golfing or tending to the property and the vines, but in the winter I have less to do. This book was written over the winter of 2017–18. I would sit on my couch after Sheila left for work and let the conversation flow from my heart and soul out to you, the reader. My thoughts and inspiration came quickly, and I felt the Holy Spirit right there beside me, letting me know what the world needed to hear.

I finished the initial draft prior to the spring of 2018, and the pictures you see in the book were taken during the course of my 2018 season in the vineyard. Somewhere in this book, I also mention that a normal harvest for me yields about four hundred fifty pounds of fruit. Well, God was ready to teach me one last lesson from the vines! In 2018, the vines were firing on all cylinders. Disease was in check and there were minimal pest invasions. My little vineyard that year produced 1,013 pounds of fruit!

The final lesson is this: don't underestimate God, ever. And don't try to set a limit to what He's capable of doing. He's much bigger and more powerful than we can imagine. A God that can be put in a box isn't much of a God, and our God will not be restrained or limited. He's the Vine and we are the branches.

Well, branches have a job to do. They bear fruit. I hope and pray that you will be inspired in your understanding of your role as a branch and fruit-bearer, and in the end that you will be ready for the harvest.

The day is coming… will you be ready?

Chapter One
The Last Lesson

Jesus Christ, who is God incarnate, meaning that He put on human skin and walked among us, both fully God and fully man, had one last lesson to teach the disciples before He went to His death on the cross, and for this lesson He chose to use the metaphor of the grape vine—to illustrate the nature of the Father and how we are to live as Christians in the world.

Welcome to my vineyard.

The passage is found in the book of John. Jesus had just partaken of the Last Supper in the upper room with the disciples, and Judas had been identified as the betrayer and fled. Jesus had already predicted Peter's denial of Him, and then He had washed the feet of the disciples and explained the coming of the Holy Spirit. He had told the disciples that He had to leave in order for the Holy Spirit to come, and that the Spirit would teach them things and remind them of what He had told them.

With this, Jesus said, *"Come now; let us leave"* (John 14:31).

They left the upper room and walked towards the Garden of Gethsemane where Jesus would later be arrested and ultimately taken for crucifixion.

But let us imagine that as they walk, they pass through a vineyard. Now, Scripture doesn't say this specifically, but it's nice to imagine that Jesus is actually standing in a vineyard. He begins to speak about grapes and vineyards, a subject which pretty much all the disciples and members of the early church would have understood. Due to sketchy water quality back then, wine was very important to the people.

His lesson went like this:

I am the true vine, and my Father is the gardener. He cuts off every branch in me that bears no fruit, while every branch that does bear fruit he prunes so that it will be even more fruitful. You are already clean because of the word I have spoken to you. Remain in me, as I also remain in you. No branch can bear fruit by itself; it must remain in the vine. Neither can you bear fruit unless you remain in me.

I am the vine; you are the branches. If you remain in me and I in you, you will bear much fruit; apart from me you can do nothing. If you do not remain in me, you are like a branch that is thrown away and withers; such branches are picked up, thrown into the fire and burned. If you remain in me and my words remain in you, ask whatever you wish, and it will be done for you. This is to my Father's glory, that you bear much fruit, showing yourselves to be my disciples.

As the Father has loved me, so have I loved you. Now remain in my love. If you keep my commands, you will remain in my love, just as I have kept my Father's commands and remain in his love. I have told you this so that my joy may be in you and that your joy may be complete. My command is this: Love each other as I have loved you. Greater love has no one than this: to lay down one's life for one's friends. You are my friends if you do what I command. I no longer call you servants, because a servant does not know his master's business. Instead, I have called you friends, for everything that I learned from my Father I have made known to you. You did not choose me, but I chose you and appointed you so that you might go and bear fruit—fruit that will last—and so that whatever you ask in my name the Father will give you. This is my command: Love each other. (John 15:1–17)

Now, Jesus could have picked any number of other images as they walked together—olive trees, other fruit trees, bees, flowers, buildings, water, clouds, the sky… yet He chose the grape vine. That has intrigued me for years, and it wasn't until I actually began planting and tending my own vineyard that this passage and its lessons sprang to life.

I want to share some of those insights in the hope that one of a number of things might happen:

1. You gain a new insight into the character of God which causes you to develop a deeper love and connection with Him.
2. You gain an insight into how the world operates which helps you face some of life's challenges.
3. You gain a renewed love for the majesty and mystery of the Trinity—the Father, Son, and Holy Spirit.
4. You gain an interest in reading the Bible a little bit differently, meaning that you begin to filter the things you experience in your world through Scripture.
5. You begin to see that we can discover God through His creation, meaning that the fingerprints of the Creator and His characteristics can be discovered in observing the things He has made—which is everything.

6. Lastly, you learn a thing or three about grapes, grape vines, and how to take care of a vineyard—if you feel so inclined to start one of your own. Crazier things have happened!

So Jesus was going to His death and then He stopped to teach His disciples one final lesson. This is akin to a dying declaration. Like, if you only had a few moments left and you knew it, you would want your last words to mean something. It would be something important, something we should pay close attention to.

Well, over the years I've discovered that this last lesson really *is* important. It's rich, deep, and full of meaning. In typical Jesus style, Him being a master communicator and all, it now takes us entire books and novels and commentaries to mine the depths of knowledge He imparted in just a few sentences.

In this case, He uttered twenty sentences. And it's going to take many, many pages to explain what I have learned from them.

That's the amazing thing about the Bible. Read it today and you gain one insight. Read it another day, and a new truth is brought to light. Sometimes it depends on our frame of mind, or the season we're in. That's why we call it the Living Word. It meets us in new and powerful ways on a daily basis. Truths or understandings we may not be ready for in one season may become crystal clear and vibrant in another. The Holy Spirit is ready to guide and instruct us, and to teach us the lessons we need to learn in order to become more like Jesus, at the time when we're finally ready to understand and accept the truth.

My understanding of this lesson wouldn't be as personal and deep if I hadn't began tending my own vineyard fifteen years ago. At the time, I wasn't a gardener or farmer by any stretch of the imagination. In fact, the extent of my gardening experience was weeding the odd flowerbed and mowing the grass.

But I had some attraction to farming in my DNA. My mother's father had been a dairy farmer, and I remembered visiting his farm and helping with the odd chore here and there.

Ultimately, however, I was a city boy.

My mother loved her gardens and had quite a flare for gardening, and by default I provided free yard care. The funny thing is, when I married Sheila, my wife of more than thirty years, I found that she was very similar to my mother. Sheila's grandpa, too, had been a farmer, and so had her dad. She had these crazy, wicked gardening skills that I had no real appreciation for—until she tricked me into moving to the country.

For the first ten years of our marriage, we lived in a small, 1,500-square-foot house in a residential subdivision. We had flower-beds in the front and back and a small yard I could cut and manicure in less than thirty minutes... "sheer" heaven, I tell you!

Little did I know that my darling bride was unhappy in this setting, that she felt claustrophobic living in such close proximity to our neighbours. She hadn't grown up having the neighbour's house literally eight feet away. She was used to being a few acres away from the nearest neighbour. She needed room to breathe... the scenery and sky... trees and vistas. Not walls, windows, driveways, and shared fences.

One day, Sheila suggested that we go for a bike ride into the country. I had no need to be suspicious of this, because we were into cycling and had gone on these sorts of rides before. But today was a little different. I had no idea that today was actually a house-hunting expedition!

As we got into the countryside, Sheila stopped in front of a beautiful, tree-lined property with a huge pond out by the road and a long, winding laneway. A majestic old farmhouse was nestled in the back, off the road. There was even a fenced pasture for horses. It was peaceful and quite nice to look at, but I already had a home.

Or at least that's what I thought.

Somehow, with manipulation, reason, and some simple arithmetic, Sheila convinced me that selling our city house and moving out to this country setting would be great for us. The housing market had recently gone through a decline, so we would take a little bit of a loss on our current house, but the asking price of the country property had also come way down.

In a way, you could look at the move as killing two birds with one stone. Sheila and I had been talking about buying a cottage up north, like so many other people we knew had done. Sheila quickly pointed out to me that if we did this I would end up spending my weekends at the cottage. I'd be taking care of two properties instead of one. That didn't sound like a lot of fun. But moving to the country was almost like having your primary residence and vacation home in one setting. Driving down this isolated laneway did provide the kind of natural tranquillity I found appealing, and I wouldn't need to drive for more than two hours to get there.

Granted, I wouldn't have that huge lakefront or a dock, but the pond was big enough to gaze out over, and it attracted some interesting wildlife, including muskrats, ferrets, blue herons, turtles, and coyotes. As a bonus, it was even stocked with some fish! So I could walk down there and do some fishing in the spring, summer, and fall. And I would clear the pond in winter for skating and the odd game of shinny—that's hockey, minus a lot of pads.

So we ended up moving out to the country.

The property was twenty-five acres. The house, pond, woods, and horse pasture sat on the front seven acres, and we rented the back eighteen acres to a local farmer. It was a lot of land, but my dear wife also found a way to turn this into a selling feature. You see, because we were registered as an active farm, we got a property tax break. Ultimately, I paid less tax on my country estate than I had in the city. That Sheila… she's a smart one!

But I had a rude awakening when I began to realize that maintaining the property had turned into a second job. Cutting the grass no longer took thirty minutes. Now it took six hours! And taking out the garbage wasn't fifteen paces from the garage to the curb… it was a three-hundred-meter hike! You certainly get your steps in when living in the country.

I also became proficient at stacking and hauling firewood. You see, this dream house we'd moved into was one hundred thirty-five years old and had been built before the dawn of electricity, indoor plumbing, and modern insulation. Their idea of insulation back then was triple brick walls and an extra layer or two of clay. To put it bluntly, the house was drafty.

When Sheila and I had an assessment done on the house's energy efficiency, the technician performed a test to determine how much air was escaping in the form of heat loss. He then sat down with us and said, "I have been doing this now for twenty years, and yours is the worst house I've ever done!"

Congratulations to us!

"Normally, the houses we deal with have a score of fifty to sixty," he continued, "and we try to get them up to seventy or eighty. Your score is thirteen! It's like you have a two-and-a-half-foot hole in the side of your house with heat leaking out constantly."

And that, ladies and gentlemen, is why I've become so proficient at stacking and hauling firewood! We have a woodstove in the main family room, and trust me when I tell you that I keep that thing stoked and humming most of my waking hours in the winter.

But I didn't set out to share my heating woes with you. I want to share about how I became a grape farmer, and how it really came about by osmosis. Osmosis is a process by which a thinner liquid is attracted to a thicker, denser liquid—in this case, my brain was the thicker, denser liquid.

I hadn't anticipated that Sheila's plan to move to the country had ultimately been about creating a vegetable garden. That was a great idea! Back-to-nature, self-sustaining stuff, right? Well, I learned that Sheila's great ideas tended to result in more manual labour for Todd.

Now, don't get me wrong. Sheila works very hard at her vegetable garden. She does her research. She does companion planting. For instance, did you know that if you plant radishes beside your cucumbers, you won't get cucumber beetles?[2] In the early spring, she plants cold weather vegetables such as peas, lettuce, spinach, and green onions. She will also rotate the potato and tomato plantings to different locations every year. But at the beginning of every year, the soil needs to be rototilled and infused with about one ton of compost. That's a Todd job!

---

[2] Not even cucumber beetles like radishes. Does anyone?

Did I mention the hauling of water from the pond to the rain barrels located by the garden? Yes, in times of drought, we need to irrigate. There are a couple of mitigating factors, though. One, we're on a well and we certainly don't want to waste our well water when we have alternatives. Two, the well water is very cold! Sheila worries that its cold temperature will shock the plants' roots. Natural rainwater is healthier for the plants anyhow. This translates to me having to take 110 steps from the pond to the rain barrel all the while carrying two full five-gallon pails, which are roughly forty-eight pounds each. This water is chock full of all sorts of composted wonderment. It takes ten pails to fill a single rain barrel. I do it because I love her, and it keeps me in shape.

But somewhere along the way, during my endless hours of mowing, stacking wood, and hauling water, the thought crept into my mind that if I was going to be doing this activity anyhow I should get something out of it. You know, if you can't beat 'em... join 'em.

I started to think, what would I be interested in growing? It didn't take me too long to come up with an answer. How about grapes for making wine?

Now, understand that we don't live in what you'd think of as wine country. This isn't California. The closest thing to wine country nearby is the Niagara region, a beautiful micro-climate about a hundred kilometres south of us. Warmed and regulated by Lake Ontario and protected by an escarpment, Niagara is a well-known, award-winning area for wineries.

But we live in Caledon, Ontario—known more for clay soil and cold weather. Was this actually a smart idea?

Well, I had a bit of a hint. When we'd moved to the property, there had been a number of old apple trees still fruiting on the land, as well as a trellised grape vine outside the front door. So clearly grapes and fruit could grow here. Secondly, an award-winning amateur vintner, Klaus, went to our church. I asked him if this would be a good idea and then suggested that we form an alliance of sorts—I grow the grapes and he makes the wine. A partnership was born!

Klaus recommended that we try growing an American hybrid variety called Foch, as it was pretty good for the temperature in our area, and fairly disease-resistant. A good indicator was that Klaus already had a number of Foch vines growing in his own backyard. So Klaus started twenty-one vines from cuttings he took from his vines during his annual pruning, and he propagated them in starter pots. Once they had formed root structures, he brought them up to our property and we planted the little darlings along the fence line by the horse pasture.

Those little vines took off! They loved it there!

Klaus taught me a lot about how to care for the vines and I began to do a ton of reading and obsessing, all in the name of research. We continued to propagate the vines using the cuttings that came from pruning. We did this every year until I had five trellis rows of approximately one hundred fifty vines.

Sheila's father helped me build the trellis lines with cedar posts and twelve-gauge wire. I had shared a vision with him of what it would look like, and then I made a sketch of how it would be laid out. One spring, my father-in-law showed up with a van full of cedar posts, a post hole digger, dozens of eight-foot metal stakes, a stake pounder, galvanized wire, wire tensioners, and earth screws. Everything I needed to fulfill the vision, he sourced the material and helped me put it together. Watching him twist the wire was amazing. I mean, he had probably done that hundreds of times, but to me it was a miracle.

I now have approximately one hundred fifty Foch vines which produce red wine, and approximately fifty Seyval Blanc vines which produce a white variety for Sheila because she doesn't like red wine. She said that if I was going to do this, she should get some enjoyment out of it as well. Fair is fair. Happy wife, happy life!

You may be starting to wonder what this has to do with my faith, so let's return to the story of the vine and branches. I don't know too many card-carrying Christians who aren't familiar with these words: *"I am the vine; you are the branches"* (John 15:5). This verse has taken on a new life for me. What I saw in my vineyard, what I saw the plants do, and what I learned about caring for it all revealed more to me each day.

In Jesus's lesson about the vine, He said that God is the gardener—some translations use the term "vinekeeper"—which means God is the orchestrator. He's the one actively organizing, planning, planting, tending, and caring for the vines to ultimately produce fruit.

Fruit which will last.

Harvest Time

A seventeenth-century Carmelite monk by the name of Brother Lawrence became renowned for experiencing profound peace despite his low station in life, working in the kitchens of a monastery. A book was later written about his life, called *The Practice of the Presence of God*. In it, Lawrence explained that his sense of peace came from openly and purposefully looking for God in all of his activities, and discovering that God would meet him there. In this way, he experienced God's presence constantly.

I found God in my vineyard, through the act of gardening and the plants themselves.

1. When was the last time you noticed God in an activity? What kind of activity was it? When you experience God in an activity, is it the same activity, or does it vary? Do you actively ask God to reveal Himself to you in all the activities you partake of in a day?
2. Do you feel there are some things too mundane or routine for God to be interested in? If yes, why do you feel that way?
3. Read Psalm 139. Make a list of what God knows. (Don't answer "Everything.")
4. For the next twenty-four to forty-eight hours, make a diary of your daily events and research scriptures that either spring to mind or that suit those events. You can search the Bible online by keyword (using tools such as www.biblegateway.com). Is this something that could become a regular practice for you? Do you feel you can find God in all that you say and do?

Chapter Two
Planning and Planting

One of the key things you need to do before getting started on a vineyard is to assess the environment for growth. A few things need to be taken into consideration.

First, what temperature zone are you in? What's the highest temperature? More importantly, what's the lowest temperature? A lot of vines can deal with high temperatures, but cold is a stressor. They can withstand some pretty cold temperatures—even as low as –25°C for a stretch—but if it stays too cold for too long, they'll have a hard time surviving.

Some growers will take their vines off the trellises at the end of the season, lay them on the ground, and cover them with soil and mulch to protect them. That's a lot of extra work, but if you're dead-set on forcing a certain variety to grow in a colder area than the vine really likes, you may have to consider this. Too much work for me!

Second, how much rainfall do you get? The secret here is generally that you want it to be a little drier versus too wet. Grape vines are amazingly hardy and have root structures that go surprisingly deep. Some of the books I've read say that roots can go down fifteen to twenty feet. I've also read that vines on hillsides in France and Germany stretch their roots hundreds of feet to reach a water source.

A lot of grapes don't do well in really wet conditions and standing water. Many gardeners would call that "wet feet." I don't like to have wet feet, and neither do your grape vines. They need to have a decent amount of rain—just not too much—and decent drainage.

Having said that, there are certain varieties that can tolerate wetter conditions and poorer drainage. My Foch, for instance, can handle soggy conditions, but they can also tolerate very dry conditions. We've seen summers in southern Ontario where there's been scorching temperatures and no rain for over a month. During our most recent drought, in 2016, I knocked myself out trying to water Sheila's vegetable garden—remember those 110 steps from the pond? We had no peas, only a few beans, the potatoes were small, and not a raspberry to be had. The Foch, however? It was one of my best years ever!

Third, consider the amount of sunshine you get and the length of the growing season. The further north you go, the longer the sun stays up during the summer. I've travelled into parts of Scotland where it was as bright as noon at 11:30 p.m., and you have to draw the blinds at night to make it dark enough to sleep. The problem there, however, is the length of the growing season. Generally it's colder and the season shorter. Ideally you need to be in an area that has a long enough growing season to allow your variety of vine to bud, flower, grow fruit, and ripen to harvest.

Fourth, give some thought to the orientation and location of your vine rows. You want your vines to be oriented in an east-west pattern so that they get the maximum amount of sunlight. You also want to plant your vines on higher ground rather than lower, if possible, because colder air sinks, and planting on low ground can lead to your new buds and flowers getting injured in the case of late spring frosts.

I've suffered the heartache of losing almost an entire season due to a late frost. It came after the vines had budded out and developed their fruiting flowers. Big operations have huge diesel air fans to move air around during a frost, but smaller home growers just have to hope and pray. It builds character!

This has all taught me that farmers are made of very strong stuff. If you're going to panic or cry over the weather, don't take up farming. You'll be chugging Prozac in no time.

Finally, you need to take a look at your soil type. Is it sandy? Loamy? Clay? Again, different vines will grow better in certain soils. If your soil is too clay-like, you could add sand. Some books suggest performing PH tests to determine soil acidity. If you want to go down that road, knock yourself out.

But here's what I learned during a recent trip to France, one of the best-known wine regions in the world. During our tour of the country, we had the privilege of stopping at Chateauneuf du Pape. This is one of the most renowned wine-producing vineyards in existence, and I was so excited to go there. I had been expecting deep, rich, manicured soil. When I got there, I found that the soil was so rocky, stony, and uninhabitable that you'd wonder how anything could grow. It was then explained to us that the soil has a unique combination of minerals that give the wine its wonderful taste and texture. You see, there's a love affair between the vines and the stones in the soil. During the day, the stones heat up from the rays from the sun, and this keeps the roots warm during the cool nights. Very romantic!

I'll stop here before moving on, because I may be scaring a few of you off. Bottom line? Go for it! I had no sense of what I was doing when I started. The majority of my vines are actually oriented northeast to southwest. Why? Because that was the direction of the pasture fence on our property. My soil? Mostly heavy clay. Did I mention the area we live in is known for having clay brick factories? All this heavy clay also leads to poor drainage. I did take some of this into consideration before planting, and that's why we chose the Foch variety.

All I'm really getting at is that unless you're looking to start a commercial vineyard, don't panic. You have to remember that grape vines are very hardy, and they can take a lot of punishment. It's said that the best wine is made where the vines are the most stressed.

Let me repeat that: the best wine is made where the vines are the most stressed—where they have to struggle, where it might be very dry or very cold. The best and sweetest fruit is grown in the most extreme conditions.

Why is that, you ask? Where conditions are easy, and nutrients and water plentiful, you get big, fat, watery, diluted grapes. Not great for wine-making. When the vines need to suffer and struggle, the berries are smaller, and the sugars and flavours are concentrated.

This is one of the lessons we'll return to over the course of this book. What is the purpose of suffering and enduring struggles? When life is easy, when we don't need to struggle for our faith, we can develop into fat, watery, diluted Christians. But struggles and trials produce perseverance, condensing and refining our faith.

Now let me share some wisdom with you. I once read a book that said vines do best when the ground is prepped in the fall, and then the vine planted in the spring. It's recommended that a trench is dug at least three feet deep and three feet wide, and that the soil be fully turned under so that the green on top gets a chance to compost under the soil. Then the soil freezes and gets flexed by ice, becoming aerated and broken down, until it's ready for spring planting.

I tried this with one of my rows of Seyval, and the plants did really well.

In the second row, I simply dug a hole twice as big as the root structure of the vine, and stuck 'em in the ground. Guess what! They did equally as well.

So what's the lesson here? Digging that trench required a ton of back-breaking work—and I'm a better, more chiselled man for having done it—so if you can save yourself the labour, just dig a hole and save your strength for something else.

When you're planting your vines, give them some room to grow. I generally plant mine about five feet apart, and the rows are generally seven to eight feet apart. Trust me, they can take up a lot of space, so you need to give them room to spread out. You also want to ensure that there's a weed-free area of two to three feet around the vine, which means mulching or hoeing. You want to keep the weed pressure down to eliminate the vine's competition for resources.

When you first get your vines, typically they're bare root, meaning that you need to get them in the soil quickly so the roots don't dry out. Have your vineyard planned in advance so that you know where to plant them, and have the holes pre-dug. Make sure you trim the roots so they don't bunch up and fold over each other when you place them in the holes, and ensure you trim the stem to about three buds to be balanced with the root structure—for example, if it's a small root structure, don't have two times that amount aboveground. And remember to create a moat around your new vine to ensure that rainwater is funnelled down to the roots.

Just as with planting roses, it's important to secure the soil around the roots to eliminate air pockets which can destroy your efforts. Then be sure to give the vine adequate water to ensure it's well hydrated. Babying your new plantings will be key for their first year of growth. Your mission will be to supply water, attention, and protection from rabbits, mice, deer, and weeds. Grow tubes can keep the vermin away. Hoeing and weed control will help keep the competition in check. And use a bamboo pole or a post of some kind to try to promote a straight trunk for the vine.

Now that you've got your plants in the ground, growth will start from those three to four buds that you left. The idea is to now choose the growth that seems strongest and is in the best position to develop into your main trunk. Once you've made this determination, cut off the undesirable growth so that the vine will begin to focus all its energy into the one or two strongest new branches. The idea is to get them growing upward—to "hit the top of the wire," as growers say. This will form your central vine for years and maybe decades to come.

The other thing you want to do is to remove any fruit the new vine is trying to form. Why? Again, you want to force the plant to grow deep roots and structure. Wasting energy on trying to develop fruit could limit the development of the roots and central vine.[3]

So in year one we baby the vines, offering them water, care, and attention.

Year two is quite different. In year two, the love stops! We now need to starve them. We still weed them and keep the competition and vermin away, but they must be starved of water. This forces the vines to send roots down deep and wide to support their growth.

---

[3] Some books say to let the fruit be. Their logic is that the plant will know what's best for itself, and if it can develop and sustain fruit, it will. I never wanted to take those chances. But you're the gardener and you make the rules!

There's once again no fruit in year two. This period of time is about forming the root structure and training the branch canes to sprout off the central vine—this will support your fruit production in year three.

The responsibility of being a vinekeeper is to plan not just for the current year's fruit production but to position branches for the following year. Keep in mind that fruit only grows on one-year-old wood, which means the new canes will be potential fruit-bearers for the next year.

So I've now told you a lot about planning and planting grape vines and establishing a vineyard, but what have I discovered about God through the process? Glad you asked!

Here's the first lesson: nothing is random with God. Just as you or I would carefully plan out where we position the vines, and how we lay out the structure of the rows and the different varieties, God has a full plan and careful structure for everything we see and know... and even for the things we can't see or know.

If the vineyard is a metaphor for the universe as we know it, and Jesus tells us that His Father is the Gardener, then God is the one laying out the plan. God is making the decisions about what happens in the world. He's in charge... I'm not. I'm the branch, meaning that I have no say other than to respond to the touch and direction of the Gardener.

A good example of this is found in Jeremiah with the story of the potter's clay:

> This is the word that came to Jeremiah from the Lord: "Go down to the potter's house, and there I will give you my message." So I went down to the potter's house, and I saw him working at the wheel. But the pot he was shaping from the clay was marred in his hands; so the potter formed it into another pot, shaping it as seemed best to him.
>
> Then the word of the Lord came to me. He said, "Can I not do with you, Israel, as this potter does?" declares the Lord. "Like clay in the hand of the potter, so are you in my hand, Israel. If at any time I announce that a nation or kingdom is to be uprooted, torn down and destroyed, and if that nation

I warned repents of its evil, then I will relent and not inflict on it the disaster I had planned. And if at another time I announce that a nation or kingdom is to be built up and planted, and if it does evil in my sight and does not obey me, then I will reconsider the good I had intended to do for it. (Jeremiah 18:1–10)

Just as the clay cannot impart action on its own to direct its own destiny, neither can a branch on a grape vine. The branch can only respond to the touch of the Master.

My second lesson is this: the order and design of the vineyard reveals the work of the planner, even if you don't see Him. I don't know about you, but there's something awe-inspiring about standing near a well-cared-for vineyard and seeing the rows stretch off into the horizon. The precise distances between plants and rows, the groomed manicured foliage, the trellises, the turned soil, the perfectly positioned fruit... all of these things scream out to me that someone has spent the time, energy, and effort to plan out this beautiful landscape, that someone has been hard at work tending it—and is actively tending it, even if I don't physically see him.

This to me is the picture of the invisible God. His design and perfect creation is all around us! The fingerprints of the designer tell us very plainly that this is not random. Someone has been hard at work to organize everything we know on earth, in our galaxy, in the universe. Our minds can't even fathom the ends of space, yet everything points to a designer... the Gardener in the vineyard!

The Apostle Paul wrote in Romans 1:19–20,

...since what may be known about God is plain to them, because God has made it plain to them. For since the creation of the world God's invisible qualities—his eternal power and divine nature—have been clearly seen, being understood from what has been made, so that people are without excuse.

My paraphrase: "Look around you! Look at the order and structure of what has been made... the trees, mountains, streams, and animals. God's fingerprints are clear and plain to see. You have no excuse not to believe that God exists!"

Science wants us to believe that this is a childish notion, and that everything we see has evolved, but I know from my science classes as a kid that matter can neither be created nor destroyed. That is a fundamental principle, and everything in the universe is made up of matter. Therefore, it had to come from somewhere—or more importantly, someone... God! He spun all things into existence, and the orderliness of the universe indicates a strategic design. We can know God is real by looking at the beauty of His craftsmanship, and by studying the intricate interdependencies in creation that go beyond human comprehension.

And just like in the vineyard, we can see the evidence of the Gardener still at work. In Jesus's lesson to the disciples, He said, *"I am the true vine, and my Father is the gardener. He cuts off every branch in me that bears no fruit..."* (John 15:1–2) He doesn't say that the gardener has planted the vineyard and left it to grow wild. No, He says that the gardener is actively tending the vineyard, and this gives me great confidence that God is still active and in charge. Nothing is random, and He still cares!

It has always been a mystery to me that more scientists don't acknowledge the existence of God, since they can see the evidence of the designer in the workings of creation. People have used the analogy of a watchmaker. If you take apart a watch and see its delicate pieces, you know that there is no way these random cogs, gears, and wheels could have fallen into a blender and resulted in this majestic timepiece. No, your conclusion must be that there is a watchmaker. There is a designer with the forethought and intelligence to fit the pieces together. You can make this deduction with a high degree of confidence even if you never meet, see, or shake hands with the watchmaker.

I think if I were a scientist looking under the hood of God's creation, I would have to appreciate the sheer elegance of the design, and therefore the designer. But alas, I am only a lowly vinekeeper. Yet I see the work of the Master Gardener all around me. Do you?

Another lesson I've learned through the planning and planting of the vineyard is the value of having healthy roots. Just as new plants need to be tended like innocent babies, new Christians need to be tended and cared for to encourage them to develop deep roots into nurturing soil.

If you've been a Christian for some time, perhaps you can think back to when you first believed and received the fresh revelatory excitement of coming to faith and meeting this wonderful Saviour named Jesus. God seemed to be everywhere. Truths seemed to leap off the page when reading the Bible. Your faith was exciting! That, to me, is like the Spirit watering, tending, and caring for our new roots.

But remember that the second year is about starving the vines to force them to search out water and nutrients for themselves. They have to grow their own strong roots. This is like those times when you hear only silence from God. Some have called it the "dark night of the soul," the period when revelation doesn't seem to come as frequently. You read your Bible, but new truths comes less and less frequently. You must press on to search for God, developing your roots and going deeper.

This process of vine training has helped me to weather the storms of life and understand the silences. I've come to see that God wants us to grow deeper roots in our faith, because we will have trials. It's not *if*, but *when*. As Jesus said, *"I have told you these things, so that in me you may have peace. In this world you will have trouble. But take heart! I have overcome the world"* (John 16:33, emphasis added).

I once heard a great quote that goes like this: "In life, we are either in the midst of a storm, coming out of a storm, or there's a storm a-comin'!" It's so true. Either we're currently going through a dark valley and in the midst of a storm, or we see light at the end of the tunnel and we're coming out of a storm. Or we're enjoying victory and times are good! In those times of victory, though, remember and be assured that a storm is a-comin'. The good times don't go on forever.

Our good and gracious Father, the vinekeeper, tries to prepare us by testing our faith, by removing the easy nourishment. He starts by giving us gentle care, perhaps in the form of surrounding us with other encouragement so we can spur one another on, but at some point we need to grow our own faith—our own roots.

Does this make God some kind of child abuser? The way I talk about starving roots, you might think so. It's like God took us to the mall when we were two years old and left us stranded. Please understand what I'm saying. I believe that God does make us struggle for our faith. There has to come a time when our beliefs are tested, or it wouldn't be called faith.

Think about it. Even Jesus went into the desert for forty days to be tested by Satan. And how did Jesus deal with that test? He quoted scripture back to Satan to shut him down. That's what it looks like to have deep roots, my friends! When the test and tempest comes, will you turn your back on God and say, "If you loved me, you would have been there"? Instead say, "God is the rock. He never changes. Bad times may come and go, but God is forever. If I have doubt, it's because of my change, not His. My roots are deep. I will cling to the rock!"

Perhaps some of you recall the parable Jesus told of the man who built his house on sand versus the man who built his house on the rock.

Why do you call me, "Lord, Lord," and do not do what I say? As for everyone who comes to me and hears my words and puts them into practice, I will show you what they are like. They are like a man building a house, who dug down deep and laid the foundation on rock. When a flood came, the torrent struck that house but could not shake it, because it was well built. But the one who hears my words and does not put them into practice is like a man who built a house on the ground without a foundation. The moment the torrent struck that house, it collapsed and its destruction was complete. (Luke 6:46–49)

Note that Jesus isn't saying you should build a solid house on a strong foundation *in case of* trial. He's saying that the trial *will* come.

In the end, here are my key takeaways:

- I can have confidence that there's a master planner and designer who's actively working and tending His creation. Why? Because I can see the orderly nature of His work. I can also have confidence that the Gardener has nothing but good intent to grow and harvest good fruit, and therefore the decisions of the Gardener are good even if I don't necessarily see the full plan.
- This helps me to understand the trying events of my life which I may not feel are warranted or fair. I need to lean into the Gardener and trust that there's a plan and that the plan is moving forward, yet the Gardener is still tending me in my struggle.
- I also can gain an understanding of periods of God's silence, when my spiritual vitality is low and God seems far off. I see the value in stressing my roots to help me build character and search for God and anchor myself to the rock. I can understand that this is part of my growth, not God being mad at me for something I've done.
- God wants us to go deeper—and we *need* to go deeper, because life will have trials. Life will have storms. Often we don't see the reality of this in our plush North American homes. We live in the opulent land of plenty. Go on a mission trip sometime. I have been on five missions. If you experience true poverty in a third-world country, you'll never complain again about what you don't have. You are blessed! But of course you are blessed to be a blessing to others, so if you haven't already done so, volunteer someplace working with the underprivileged. Or at least give to a charity.[4]

Harvest Time

1. Consider the statement, "The best wine is made where the vines are the most stressed." List the five most stressful events that have happened in your life—times when you had to struggle,

---

[4] I suggest you check out www.risingangels.net. But I digress!

strive, and work hard. How did they change you? How did you meet God in the process?

2. Read Jeremiah 18:1–10. Describe how you feel about the way in which God is forming your life in His hands. What kind of person were you before you met Christ and how have you changed? Do you feel you are "mouldable" clay, or do you feel as though you are fighting change? Why?

3. Write out at least three examples of how you know that God is still actively working in the world. How does this make you feel?

4. Have you experienced "the dark night of the soul," times when God seems to have withdrawn from you? How has this changed you? Has your faith grown deeper or grown weaker?

5. In the storm analogy, you are either experiencing a storm (times are tough), coming out of a storm (the battle is over and times are getting better), or there's a storm a-comin' (times are easy but tough times are on the way). Describe where you are now. How is God working with you or shaping you to deal with what's coming? Do you think it's fair that God treats us this way?

Chapter Three
Pruning

One of my key activities year in year out is pruning, which is the purposeful planning, selection, and cutting of the plant growth every year to promote health. It's an educated and creative decision that must be made on what to keep and what to throw away, just like in Jesus's lesson to the disciples when He said, *"He cuts off every branch in me that bears no fruit, while every branch that does bear fruit he prunes so that it will be even more fruitful"* (John 15:2).

Vines before pruning.

Vines after pruning.

Pruning cuttings ready for the fire.

That is what I do every spring. I go out into the vineyard and assess each vine. What am I looking for? The first thing to understand about grape vines is that they are prolific growers. But I look to keep only four to five well positioned, vigorous one-year-old canes each year, canes that are in close proximity to the main vine and are oriented in the right direction so as to be highly trainable on the trellis lines.

Let me break this down for you.

In any given year, I'll cut back and prune approximately ninety percent of a vine's growth from the previous year. As I said, I only want four to five canes on a vine so as not to stress the main vine. I want to limit growth so that the vine puts all its efforts into producing a manageable amount of fruit versus trying to produce too much and getting poor quality fruit. Remember: the Gardener is all about the plan to produce the best fruit!

Now, I also mentioned one-year-old canes. Did you know that fruit only grows on one-year-old wood? Yep! The canes I look for, the ones that will produce good fruit, are the ones that were new the previous year. Canes that had fruit on them the previous year will have created fruiting buds from the last growing season. But in the third year, these canes become barren.

I vigorously search for old wood to cut out, because it's useless to me in terms of growing fruit. Similarly, the Master Gardener is looking to weed out the deadwood that won't contribute good fruit. The deadwood in your life won't produce the good fruit of the kingdom and has to go! What is deadwood? Think of any habits, behaviours, or attitudes that don't support God's plan. You can probably already list several things God would want to prune out of you. Let Him do His work. He knows what He's doing!

I then look to ensure that the fruiting branch is positioned as close to the main vine as possible, because it keeps the vines from spreading and crowding out other vines. Also, the canes nearest the main vine are stronger and better nourished. Did Jesus not say that He is the vine and we are the branches? We are connected to the vine, and the ones closest to the vine are best positioned to be nourished and bear good fruit. The further I get from the main vine, the lesser the quality of my fruit. Why? Because Jesus said that we can do nothing apart from Him. If I'm connected to the vine but positioned further away, I can still produce fruit… it just might be of poorer quality.[5]

I'm also looking for canes that are pointed in the right direction along the trellis lines, which means that when they start to produce new growth it will be easier to manage. A cane may look really nice—it might have the right diameter (about the size of a pencil) and nice-looking fruit buds—but it may be pointed in the wrong direction, which isn't favourable for growth. Once the new growth starts, it will produce more weight than the cane can support, and the cane will snap. Trust me… I know from experience. These vines will grow well beyond their capacity to support themselves, so they need to be tied to a trellis and trimmed regularly. We never want vines to lie on the ground, because that will make them more susceptible to disease.

This causes me to stop and think about my own life. We as human beings are resilient, talented, resourceful, intelligent, and can achieve much on our own. Consider the story about the tower of Babel:

---

[5] Remember that even in the parable of the talents, there was a middle servant who received two talents and grew them to four. This was still a good return, but not as good as the servant who was given five and grew it to ten.

Now the whole world had one language and a common speech. As people moved eastward, they found a plain in Shinar[b] and settled there.

They said to each other, "Come, let's make bricks and bake them thoroughly." They used brick instead of stone, and tar for mortar. Then they said, "Come, let us build ourselves a city, with a tower that reaches to the heavens, so that we may make a name for ourselves; otherwise we will be scattered over the face of the whole earth."

But the Lord came down to see the city and the tower the people were building. The Lord said, "If as one people speaking the same language they have begun to do this, then nothing they plan to do will be impossible for them. Come, let us go down and confuse their language so they will not understand each other."

So the Lord scattered them from there over all the earth, and they stopped building the city. (Genesis 11:1–8)

Essentially, humankind was going to glorify themselves as gods and build a tower that reached the heavens, all to make a name for themselves. I think today we have a saying for this: going rogue, meaning that we're in it for ourselves—for our own glory, our own fame. Notice that God said, *"If as one people speaking the same language they have begun to do this, then nothing they plan to do will be impossible for them"* (Genesis 11:6).

The same is true of ill-positioned rogue vines that insist on going out on their own strength. They can achieve much, but eventually their success causes them to bend under their own weight. In some cases, they droop to the ground and become prone to disease, and in other cases they break off and detach from the vine.

The lesson is clear: we can achieve much on our own, but unless we're trainable and remain close to the vine, we run a risk of being defeated by our own success.

What are your personal successes? What are you proud of? What have you achieved under your own strength apart from God...

apart from the vine? Newsflash: this isn't fruit that lasts, and it could eventually be your downfall.

Consider what Paul says:

...though I myself have reasons for such confidence.

If someone else thinks they have reasons to put confidence in the flesh, I have more: circumcised on the eighth day, of the people of Israel, of the tribe of Benjamin, a Hebrew of Hebrews; in regard to the law, a Pharisee; as for zeal, persecuting the church; as for righteousness based on the law, faultless.

But whatever were gains to me I now consider loss for the sake of Christ. What is more, I consider everything a loss because of the surpassing worth of knowing Christ Jesus my Lord, for whose sake I have lost all things. I consider them garbage, that I may gain Christ and be found in him, not having a righteousness of my own that comes from the law, but that which is through faith in Christ—the righteousness that comes from God on the basis of faith. I want to know Christ—yes, to know the power of his resurrection and participation in his sufferings, becoming like him in his death, and so, somehow, attaining to the resurrection from the dead. (Philippians 3:4–11)

He considered everything he'd accomplished to be garbage. His credentials, by worldly standards, were worth nothing compared to knowing and following Jesus Christ. Here is someone who knew the meaning of staying close to the vine and realizing that he could do nothing of kingdom value apart from it.

Yes, we can achieve a lot. God made us that way! David wrote, "I am fearfully and wonderfully made" (Psalm 149:14). But his son Solomon later wrote, "Yet when I surveyed all that my hands had done and what I had toiled to achieve, everything was meaningless, a chasing after the wind; nothing was gained under the sun" (Ecclesiastes 2:11).

There are three main points to this. Number one, stay rooted to the vine, Jesus. Two, your achievements in kingdom work are the things that matter. That's the fruit God is looking for. And finally, be careful about where you invest your time and effort. Are you chasing the wind, investing in something that's self-serving? Don't be defeated by your own success.

The whole act of pruning is an exercise in tough love. I must be ruthless for the sake of the quality of fruit to be produced. I must relentlessly analyze each vine and select the best canes to keep, cutting away anything that will hinder that goal. This includes cutting away deadwood, canes that appear diseased, and canes that are low to the ground or in a bad position.

But this isn't as simple as cutting just for the sake of cutting. When I remove a one-year-old fruiting cane because it isn't in the best position, I leave two fruit buds on that cane, to act as renewal spurs. You see, by pruning I select what will produce fruit this year... but I'm also planning for the following year!

Renewal spur

I laugh to myself as I write this, because when I first started, I was so confused, so paralyzed by thinking I might make the wrong decision. I would stare at the vine, not knowing where to start. Eventually I'd move in slowly and start a game called "Not You!" It was a game of elimination, meaning I would at bare minimum choose growth that I knew had to go, and say "Not you!" Having weeded out the obvious candidates, I would then make some really hard decisions about what was left over, about who would stay and who would go.

But remember, branches don't go entirely! They can have life as a renewal spur, and perhaps bear fruit the next year.

When I first started, it could take me up to half an hour to prune a vine, because I was so paranoid about making the wrong decisions. Now it takes me about ten minutes because I quickly decide what's going to work and what isn't.

As Christians, we sometimes think we've blown it because of something we said or did, and that's it... we've lost our Christian membership card. Not true! Our God is so good, so gracious, and so merciful that He gives us second chances. And thirds, and fourths.

That's not to say we can go on sinning for the sake of sinning. Just like with a renewal spur, God deals with something in our lives by cutting it away, but He leaves behind a growth bud so we can try again.

For instance, I'm terrible at handling conflict. If you have a problem with me, or if I have a problem with you, I'll ignore it and the problem will go away. Right? Wrong! That's not how God wants us to interact with one another. He wants us to exercise conflict resolution. He wants us to show forgiveness.

Jesus told Peter that we need to forgive our brothers seven times seventy-seven, meaning infinitely. Jesus did this from the cross! And me? Can I manage to forgive someone who may have said some mean words to me? Those are hardly nails in the hands and feet. So God keeps working with me. He leaves a renewal spur so I can try again and hopefully get better at relationships. Trust me, I still suck at them, but I think I'm getting better. Thank goodness God hasn't given up on me. The simple fact that I'm concerned about letting Him down means that the Holy Spirit isn't done with me yet. He's not done with you either.

I'd also like to mention that I wait until the vines start a process called "bud swell" before I start pruning. The bud swell is when the buds start to swell up and get ready to burst forth with growth.[6]

---

[6] They look a bit like Jiffy Pop popcorn containers after the corn has popped and foil swells up. If you're not old enough to remember the reference, look it up on YouTube!

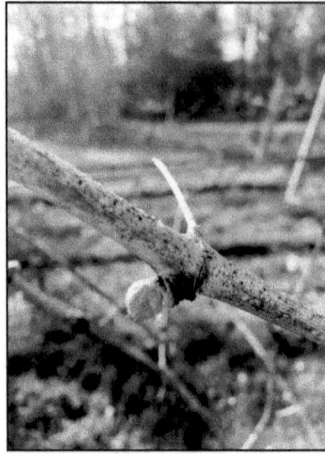

Bud swell.

The reason I wait for the bud swell is so that I can see what has survived the winter and determine what is alive. Some commercial growers will actually go out into the vineyard and take cuttings, then bring them back indoors where they'll take a razor to cut open the bud and see if it's green inside—in other words, alive. Based on the survival rate, they'll determine how many buds they should keep per cane to get the amount of fruit they want. That's a necessity for them, because when you have thousands of vines to prune you need to start in March to get the job done in time for spring. But my little vineyard is manageable, and I can afford to wait until I see what's actually alive and what isn't.

After we've selected our fruiting canes and cut away everything else, we've accumulated a mound of wood cuttings. Much of this is dead or diseased wood, and I'll take it to the firepit and burn it. Why? Because if there's disease in the wood, I don't want it anywhere near the vineyard. I want it eradicated and gone... permanently.

This is why I don't think it's strange when Jesus said, *"If you do not remain in me, you are like a branch that is thrown away and withers; such branches are picked up, thrown into the fire and burned"* (John 15:6). Anyone familiar with the practices of managing a vineyard would have caught His meaning.

I don't know about you, but I have things in my life—deadwood, disease of character—that need to be pruned. They can't be part of my life. They need to be burned in the fire and return no more.

"Now hold on, Todd," I can hear you thinking. "I slip and fall occasionally. Sometimes I repeat the same sin. It's not gone. Does this mean I'm not a Christian?"

No. And if you got that impression... again I say no. I'll dedicate a whole chapter ahead to the issue of disease in the vineyard, but the bottom line is that sometimes we don't get all the disease out through the cuttings and some residual disease remains in the vineyard. It's hard not to be exposed to some disease, simply by being part of the world. So we need to do our part to put on the full armour of Christ, as described in this famous writing by Paul:

> Finally, be strong in the Lord and in his mighty power. Put on the full armor of God, so that you can take your stand against the devil's schemes. For our struggle is not against flesh and blood, but against the rulers, against the authorities, against the powers of this dark world and against the spiritual forces of evil in the heavenly realms. Therefore put on the full armor of God, so that when the day of evil comes, you may be able to stand your ground, and after you have done everything, to stand. Stand firm then, with the belt of truth buckled around your waist, with the breastplate of righteousness in place, and with your feet fitted with the readiness that comes from the gospel of peace. In addition to all this, take up the shield of faith, with which you can extinguish all the flaming arrows of the evil one. Take the helmet of salvation and the sword of the Spirit, which is the word of God. (Ephesians 6:10–17)

We put on the armour of God, but sometimes we still fall—because we're works in progress. Being refined and pruned is a lifelong journey, but don't get the impression that if you fail, if you falter even once, you're done. Even in baseball, you get three strikes!

Some pastors preach a very hard message, I think a dangerous message, regarding sin being an indicator of whether you're truly saved. For example, Sheila and I were youth leaders at our church for fifteen years, and each February we would take the kids to a massive youth winter retreat where there were bands, worship, and activities galore, but also sermons and messages culminating in communion on the final night where kids gave their lives to Christ. It was an amazing event, and it was a privilege to be a part of it and to witness God's power and the moving of the Spirit.

One year, however, the keynote speaker had a very hard message. He used Jesus's parable of the sheep and the goats:

When the Son of Man comes in his glory, and all the angels with him, he will sit on his glorious throne. All the nations will be gathered before him, and he will separate the people one from another as a shepherd separates the sheep from the goats. He will put the sheep on his right and the goats on his left.

Then the King will say to those on his right, "Come, you who are blessed by my Father; take your inheritance, the kingdom prepared for you since the creation of the world. For I was hungry and you gave me something to eat, I was thirsty and you gave me something to drink, I was a stranger and you invited me in, I needed clothes and you clothed me, I was sick and you looked after me, I was in prison and you came to visit me."

Then the righteous will answer him, "Lord, when did we see you hungry and feed you, or thirsty and give you something to drink? When did we see you a stranger and invite you in, or needing clothes and clothe you? When did we see you sick or in prison and go to visit you?"

The King will reply, "Truly I tell you, whatever you did for one of the least of these brothers and sisters of mine, you did for me."

Then he will say to those on his left, "Depart from me, you who are cursed, into the eternal fire prepared for the devil and his angels. For I was hungry and you gave me nothing to eat, I was thirsty and you gave me nothing to drink, I was a stranger and you did not invite me in, I needed clothes and you did not clothe me, I was sick and in prison and you did not look after me."

They also will answer, "Lord, when did we see you hungry or thirsty or a stranger or needing clothes or sick or in prison, and did not help you?"

He will reply, "Truly I tell you, whatever you did not do for one of the least of these, you did not do for me."

Then they will go away to eternal punishment, but the righteous to eternal life. (Matthew 25:31–46)

In essence, his message to the youth that night was this: if you sin, maybe you're not as saved as you think you are and Jesus doesn't know you. Oh boy! That threw the kids for a loop, and we ended up regrouping with them afterwards to do some damage control. The kids were confused.

"But I thought Jesus loved sinners and came to heal them," they said.

It was a long night of talking it through and telling them that there is forgiveness, and that God looks at the heart and sincerity of your faith... not whether you've stumbled and sinned once, twice, or a hundred times.

We are human and we will err, and it's damaging and irresponsible, to say the least, to tell people that if you accept Christ but still sin, you're not a Christian. I was fit to be tied, and I wasn't having very Christian thoughts that night.

I think the organizers knew there could be some blowback from this, because they had the speaker come back the next morning to qualify his message. It was good for the kids to hear that, and to understand that the body of Christ works together. But I think it was also good for the speaker to see the instant impact of a message gone astray.

The last lesson in this chapter has to do with a process called propagation. I mentioned earlier that I sometimes need to cut away healthy branches that unfortunately aren't in my plans that year, but that doesn't mean these branches are totally useless. Occasionally a vine will die and need to be replaced, in which case I'll take the healthy canes and cut them into sticks with at least three healthy buds on each one. I then dip one end into a rooting hormone and plant it in the ground. This is called propagation.

There's nothing scientific or challenging about this process. As long as you keep the branch watered and weed-free, those little sticks will sprout buds, grow roots, and start a new plant. As a matter of fact, that's exactly how I populated the balance of my vines from the original supply given to me by my friend. From an original count of twenty-one vines, I propagated them into one hundred fifty. I still keep a reserve nursery of six to twelve little ones, filling in spaces every year.

My lesson in this is that nothing is wasted with God. He can use all things for His purposes.

Sometimes there are parts of my life I'm not ready to face. Perhaps it's just not the season for that particular thing, so God takes it away and parks it for another time when the season is right.

I'll give you an example. Sheila and I have a friend who desperately wants to be in a relationship with a man. Her self-worth is tied up in being desirable to a man. This stems from tragic events in her early life that saw her being raped and abused. This abuse lasted for many years. Her abuser told her how lucky she was that he had chosen her, because he was going to teach her how to take care of her man later in life. He told her that she had been chosen because she was prettier than the other girls. This deeply scarred her sense of self-worth.

Forty years later, that same need to be attractive to a man is still there—to a lesser degree now, because she's become a Christian. Slowly but surely, God is pruning her and showing her that she is loved and valuable not because of her looks, but because she is a child of the King!

In relationships, she tries to force her agenda—and God keeps shutting the door. What does "shutting the door" look like? She's beginning to see why she is attracted to the wrong men. Perhaps a man behaves towards her in an abusive way she would have accepted before, out of desperation, but she now sees it for what it is. So God isn't cutting relationships out of her life forever. The right season isn't here yet. He just wants the right relationship for her, for the right reasons, at the right time.

Maybe you've been praying for something and are getting frustrated with God's timing. Be patient. God's timing is always perfect, and His ways always right. We can't necessarily see that from our limited perspective, but this is where faith and trust must manifest themselves in our lives. If we don't believe that God is all-powerful, all-knowing, and all-seeing, and that He loves us beyond what we can comprehend, and that He proved it by going to the cross, then who are we worshipping?

Part of our growth as Christians is embracing the blessing of contentment. Paul wrote that he had learned how to be content, how to rest in Christ:

> I rejoiced greatly in the Lord that at last you renewed your concern for me. Indeed, you were concerned, but you had no opportunity to show it. I am not saying this because I am in need, for I have learned to be content whatever the circumstances. I know what it is to be in need, and I know what it is to have plenty. I have learned the secret of being content in any and every situation, whether well fed or hungry, whether living in plenty or in want. I can do all this through him who gives me strength. (Philippians 4:10–13)

We need to be knowledgeable about who God is, understand His love and care for us in our circumstances, be content in our faith, and trust that God will bring about in the right season exactly what we need in the way and timing we need it. May we rest on this blessed assurance!

I've known many people who have prayed for children who are off the rails and heading towards self-destruction. It's so hard to witness grieving parents watch their sons or daughters make bad choices and harm themselves in unspeakable ways. They pray and ask others for prayer, yet nothing seems to change. Sometimes it ends very badly for the child, even in death, and we cry out, "Where were you, God!?"

In our limited human capacity, we can never know how often God tried to help that child, yet the help was refused. In our own understanding, we cannot see all that happened behind the scenes, how many times God knocked on a closed door. We need to trust and have faith that God is who He says He is, and that He is loving—all the time.

Harvest Time

1. When pruning vines, I look for branches that are well-positioned close to the main vine. This is comparable to remaining close to Jesus. I used to play a game with our youth group, called the Restaurant Game. If you saw Jesus sitting in a restaurant, where would you be in that restaurant, in relation to Him, and why?[7]

2. You probably already have a short list of things that need to be pruned from your life, such as attitudes, habits, and behaviours. What's on your list? Where is God pruning you? How well do you respond to pruning? Has your attitude and responsiveness to God's pruning gotten better or worse over the last few years? How has your relationship with Him gotten better or worse? Is there a correlation between your relationship with God and your acceptance of His instructions?

3. Describe where you're investing your time. Do you spend it on yourself or on the kingdom? How can you know the difference? Paul considered his personal achievements to be garbage versus knowing and doing the will of Christ. Are you striving under your own power or thriving in the will of Christ? Be honest. Stop, pray, and ask God to reveal this to you.

4. What lesson does God seem to keep bringing back in front of you, like a renewal spur? What are you currently struggling with? Do you feel like it's getting better or worse? Do you fear you

---

[7] Some would answer that they were still in the parking lot, and I appreciated the honesty.

might lose your salvation or Christian status? Why or why not? How should this affect the way we live?

5. In Philippians 4:10–13, Paul wrote that he knew what it means to have plenty and to be needy, but in all things we are to be content in the love and provision of the Lord. How has God provided for you in a time of need? What are you praying for and in need of right now? Do you trust that God will provide what you need, when you need it, in the right season? How is your patience and trust?

Chapter Four
Training

Once the vines have been pruned and I've selected the fruiting canes,
it's time to sit and watch the growth begin. From a bud the size of a
raindrop, the bud swell explodes and the initial leaf and stem seem
to roll out of the branch. It would be amazing to view this process
with time-lapse photography, although I haven't done it, because the
day-to-day growth is really quite astounding. Below are a few pictures
showing the growth over the course of a few days.

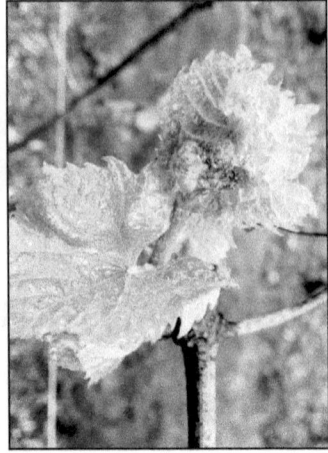

One of the first things to emerge is the flower sets, which eventually become grapes. I have to do a few things at this stage.

First, I "rub out," or flick off, any unwanted buds. Sometimes buds will emerge from the stem or main vine in places where I don't want them because they may become problematic if left to grow. This includes buds that are low to the ground, or buds facing away from the trellis, or buds that are growing into another cane or bud and they will eventually crowd each other out.

Second, I eliminate too much growth, leaving approximately seven to nine fruiting buds on a cane to ensure I'll have the volume of fruit I want, should a couple of those buds die off. This happens sometimes with late-season frosts. If there's no such die-off, I could be left with too many buds, overtaxing the vine. If that happens, I'll remove the buds that are furthest away from the vine to ensure the vine is balanced.

I'll look for new growth that has more than two flower sets. Sometimes they'll have three flowers on them, which would eventually turn into three bunches of grapes—something you don't really want. You want to eliminate the third set, the one furthest from the vine, so that the ones closest to the vine will receive the most nourishment. This means that more sugars will be pumped into them closer to harvest, which equals great fruit and good wine.

Grape flowers before bloom.

Grape flowers in bloom.

End of bloom and fruit growth begins.

Fourth, at this time of year I'll look at the overall health of the vine itself. How well has it wintered? Is the new growth strong or is it weak? Again, I have to apply tough love. There's no point leaving a sick vine in the vineyard that could end up spreading disease. If a vine is sick, I'll start by looking to see if there's any new growth coming from the ground. If there is, I might let it grow to become a new central vine, then cut the sickly central vine away. Or I may cut out the whole thing, burn it, and replace it with one of my propagated replacements. It's a matter of knowing if the disease is coming from the wood aboveground, underground, or if the vine is just old and it's time to call it a career.

I also remove suckers, outgrowths that spring up either near the ground or near to the spot where the plant may have been injured. I want to pluck these off because they sap energy that should go towards the healthy branches that produce new fruit and growth for the next year.

Now the process is about training the new growth to align itself to the trellis wire, and to encourage the new growth to attach itself to the trellis using a funky thing called a tendril. Tendrils are so cool! The grape vine is looking to climb and climb and climb, and to do that it needs to secure itself to something or it will fall due to its own weight. So the tendril's purpose is to provide something the vine can grab onto to support the oncoming growth.

The most interesting part of the grape vine is how teachable it is. I'll walk through the vineyard and guide those little tendrils to the trellis wire, hooking them on. If I go back two or three days later, I'll find that the vine has tightly wrapped itself around the wire and begun the anchoring process.

As the stem grows longer—they'll grow twenty feet in a season if you let them—I'll guide the new tendrils to the wire for support. If the vine won't grab on with a tendril, I need to attach it to the trellis wire with strings or biodegradable ties.

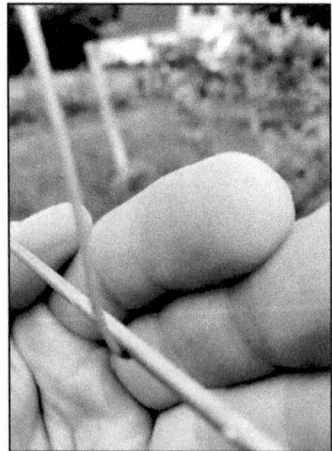

New tendril begin trained to the wire.

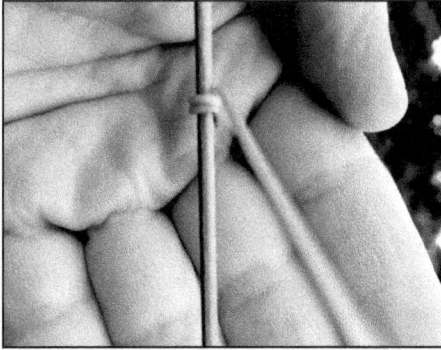

New tendril securing itself to the wire.

Here's the curious thing I've noticed about tendrils: they work better under tension! If there's a stem with a tendril close to the wire, even touching the wire, but no tension between the tendril and the wire, chances are that the tendril won't grab on. But if there is tension, the tendril will kick into high gear, grab the wire, and wrap around it.

Tendril under tension.

My biggest takeaway from these activities is that God, the Master Gardener, is all about training us into the men and women, boys and girls, He wants us to be to become. He wants to shape us into the image of His Son Jesus Christ and to prepare us for the work He has predestined for us. The Spirit is constantly looking to rub out, or flick off, the undesirable growth in our lives—those habits, traits, and attitudes about ourselves that give us a twinge in the pit of our stomachs.

Through this process, the Holy Spirit is looking to deal with small things in our lives before they become bigger problems.

Scripture says that God disciplines and chastises those He loves just as a father disciplines or chastises his children so they will grow up to be healthy and wise:

> In your struggle against sin, you have not yet resisted to the point of shedding your blood. And have you completely forgotten this word of encouragement that addresses you as a father addresses his son? It says, "My son, do not make light of the Lord's discipline, and do not lose heart when he rebukes you, because the Lord disciplines the one he loves, and he chastens everyone he accepts as his son."
>
> Endure hardship as discipline; God is treating you as his children. For what children are not disciplined by their father? If you are not disciplined—and everyone undergoes discipline—then you are not legitimate, not true sons and daughters at all. Moreover, we have all had human fathers who disciplined us and we respected them for it. How much more should we submit to the Father of spirits and live! They disciplined us for a little while as they thought best; but God disciplines us for our good, in order that we may share in his holiness. No discipline seems pleasant at the time, but painful. Later on, however, it produces a harvest of righteousness and peace for those who have been trained by it. (Hebrews 12:4–11)

In the same way, as children of God, we can expect that God will correct us when we act, say, or even think things that are contrary to His will. Do not be surprised by this. In fact, embrace it. You may have heard the old saying: "God accepts you just the way you are... but He loves you too much to leave you that way." Just as I'm going to tend my vineyard to get the best out of it, God is going to tend and train you to get the most out of you. One of the reasons we don't respond to God's training, and end up getting stuck in a faith rut, is apathy. As Jesus said to the Church in Laodicea,

To the angel of the church in Laodicea write: These are the
words of the Amen, the faithful and true witness, the ruler of
God's creation. I know your deeds, that you are neither cold
nor hot. I wish you were either one or the other! So, because
you are lukewarm—neither hot nor cold—I am about to spit
you out of my mouth. You say, "I am rich; I have acquired
wealth and do not need a thing." But you do not realize that
you are wretched, pitiful, poor, blind and naked. I counsel you
to buy from me gold refined in the fire, so you can become
rich; and white clothes to wear, so you can cover your
shameful nakedness; and salve to put on your eyes, so you
can see.

Those whom I love I rebuke and discipline. So be earnest
and repent. (Revelation 3:14–19)

These are heavy words from the gentle Lamb! Pitiful. Poor. Blind.
Naked... ouch! But He also said, *"Those whom I love I rebuke and*
discipline."

We are not to be lukewarm, which means neither hot nor cold—
neither being on fire for Jesus nor being so far away and cold that we
catch a chill. To be lukewarm means to be apathetic.

If you feel the sting of rebuke, if you feel the full weight of remorse
for the consequence of your actions, then rejoice, because God's
not done with you! Not because you got caught or found out, but
because He's God and knows what you've done. You aren't hiding
anything. Yet He disciplines you because you belong to Him. You are
His child and He is your great Father, the Master Gardener who will
train you up in the way you must go.

Let that really, really sink in. Go back and read that Revelation
3 passage a few more times. Your legitimacy as a child of the King
means that you will be disciplined. You will be humbled, shamed,
crushed, and broken.

Who understood this more in biblical history than David? If you
recall his story, he was a man after God's own heart, and God blessed
him and anointed him as king over His people.

God taught David, when he was young, to care for His people by having him work as a shepherd tending helpless sheep.[8] David fought lions and bears that tried to take his sheep. Lions and bears! Many people never catch this aspect of the story. Before God sent David to slay Goliath, He had been training him in the field. He was ready for the giant *because he had already faced giants.* What kind of Father would God be if He had sent David into a battle with no experience?

God also protected David from the mad king Saul, and David spent many years of running and fighting between the time when he was anointed king and the time when he actually became king. Again, God was building David's character, teaching and training him how to be a king, how to rule people with compassion and rule with God-fearing wisdom.

But then comes the story everybody knows. David stayed home instead of going to war with his army and had an adulterous affair with Bathsheba. Even worse, David concocted a scheme to have Bathsheba's husband Uriah murdered on the front lines of battle to cover his sin. David was then confronted by God through the prophet Nathan, and David's sin was dragged out into the light. He was caught, called to account, and disciplined. What was David's response?

Have mercy on me, O God, according to your unfailing love; according to your great compassion blot out my transgressions. Wash away all my iniquity and cleanse me from my sin.

For I know my transgressions, and my sin is always before me. Against you, you only, have I sinned and done what is evil in your sight; so you are right in your verdict and justified when you judge. Surely I was sinful at birth, sinful from the time my mother conceived me. Yet you desired faithfulness even in the womb; you taught me wisdom in that secret place.

Cleanse me with hyssop, and I will be clean; wash me, and I will be whiter than snow. Let me hear joy and gladness;

---

[8] Remember that Jesus has been described a shepherd, too, and we have been called lost sheep.

let the bones you have crushed rejoice. Hide your face from my sins and blot out all my iniquity.

Create in me a pure heart, O God, and renew a steadfast spirit within me. Do not cast me from your presence or take your Holy Spirit from me. Restore to me the joy of your salvation and grant me a willing spirit, to sustain me.

Then I will teach transgressors your ways, so that sinners will turn back to you. Deliver me from the guilt of bloodshed, O God, you who are God my Savior, and my tongue will sing of your righteousness. Open my lips, Lord, and my mouth will declare your praise. You do not delight in sacrifice, or I would bring it; you do not take pleasure in burnt offerings. My sacrifice, O God, is a broken spirit; a broken and contrite heart you, God, will not despise.

May it please you to prosper Zion, to build up the walls of Jerusalem. Then you will delight in the sacrifices of the righteous, in burnt offerings offered whole; then bulls will be offered on your altar. (Psalm 51:1–19)

David was a man experiencing pruning and training. He didn't make excuses as He felt the hand of the Master Gardener on him.

In reading Psalm 51, you can feel the weight of sin that had been upon David. David really got to the heart of it when he said, *"My sacrifice, O God, is a broken spirit; a broken and contrite heart…"* Under great tension and stress, David clung to God. David is like a tendril under tension, clinging and wrapping itself around the trellis wire.

We must come to the Father and say, "Wash me, cleanse me, restore me, sustain me." This is what it means to be trainable, to respond to the touch of the Master Gardener.

From this, we can learn some deep lessons about dealing with discipline and difficult situations. It can help us to understand God, Jesus, and the Holy Spirit in a more significant and profound way.

God trains and guides. Like branches of the vine, He tries to put us in the right position for our own good, even if it feels restrictive. Sometimes that means being bent back towards the trellis wire because we're straying from where we need to be. This happens when I exercise too much Todd power and not enough God power!

Sometimes new growth needs to be lashed to the trellis wire, and tied there for its own protection. Think of the Ten Commandments. I can't think of too many people who would say that by following the Ten Commandments they had a crap life. If anyone says that, you can tell them to call me. That would be a first.

That's because following those commandments isn't about lashing us and tying us to restrict us. The point of it is to keep us safe so that we can flourish in life and be abundant and productive. It would be like going ziplining and removing the harness because it feels too tight. Those harnesses are what make the activity safe and enjoyable!

The branch is blind. It gropes in the dark, looking for safety in the harsh reality of life. That's me... and I think that's you, too. It's all of us. We are wretched, pitiful, poor, blind, and naked, groping in the dark with our tendrils, trying to find something to grasp onto that is solid and real. Jesus said, *"I am the way and the truth and the life"* (John 14:6). God the Master Gardener directs our tendrils back to the wire—back to Christ. Do you want to have a firm foundation, something in life to count on, a sure thing? Grab onto Jesus and don't let go!

I need to be ready to have the unproductive areas of my life plucked away and removed, since they distract from the fruit of my life. I need to loosen my grip on some things, habits, and people that might not be healthy for me. How willing are we to do that? Are we trainable? Do we make excuses? Are we fooling ourselves?

Be like David, and don't delay in taking instruction once you've been confronted with your sin. The reality is that God has all the time in the world—literally. If an area in your life needs to be dealt with, it's going to be dealt with. Do you want to fight against it for years, or do you want to experience moments of humility, repentance, and peace? I'll take moments over years, please.

The company I work for has a core value that says, "Tell the truth and tell it fast." This is so true. David carried around sin, guilt, and regret, and it crushed his bones. This is what happens to us under the weight of our own selfishness and pride. So disarm your guilt and crush your shame by learning lessons fast!

God trains and disciplines the ones He loves, but it's a lifelong process that isn't going to stop. This isn't a case where you can go through a momentary painful lesson and then go into cruise control for the rest of your life. I can expect that as I go deeper in my walk with God, He will reveal new things to me that need to be dealt with. Give these areas to Him and trust Him in their care.

Blind tendril searching for something to secure to,
groping in the wind.

A few years back, when Sheila and I were youth leaders, one of the girls attending our youth group was a sweet, angelic girl named Deidre. Deidre and Sheila became very close, and over time we learned that Deidre's mother was actively involved in prostitution. We got to meet Deidre's mother, Katarina, when Sheila and I hosted a birthday party at our house for Deidre. This was the first time I met Kat. She was a striking figure, to say the least. She had about a hundred tattoos, and together with her black hair it sent a real message: "Don't mess with me." It was curious how Kat and this sweet Christian girl Deidre could even be related, but they were.

How had Kat entered prostitution? She now tells the story on speaking tours, but here's the short version. She was raped from the age of two[9] by a family member. There were warning signs something was wrong but no one asked questions. After her parents divorced when Kat was 9, she had no male figure in her life. She started acting out and became promiscuous, looking for affection. She then became pregnant at the age of fourteen—and that daughter was Deidre.

Over the years, Kat endured many abusive relationships, but she didn't know they were abusive because she had been damaged starting at the age of two. Because of her abuse, she had a warped sense of what was normal.

She later married a man who was abusive and a criminal, going in and out of jail. One of her husband's friends, murdered her husband and basically kept Kat, her mother, and her family hostage for the next three years. They weren't hostages under lock and key, but there were threats against her and her children. It was a type of mental confinement.

To throw police off the trail, the murderer suggested that Kat attend a support group for abused women. There, Kat met a lady who offered her a job at a massage parlour. That woman ended up being the ex-girlfriend of the murderer's father.[10] Kat figured if she could work and save money, she could escape the abuse. She had no other alternatives, so the trap was set.

As time went on, Sheila and I heard occasional news from Deidre about Kat, and we eventually learned that she had left prostitution and was now living with a man. This man had apparently "rescued" Kat from prostitution. He had been a regular customer of hers and convinced her to leave the industry so he could take care of her and her children. In the end, though, it turned out that he was really just revictimizing her, and keeping her on as his own private prostitute. At one point, he had even suggested she start a porn website to help make extra money. You can imagine how devastating that was to

---

[9] Eighty-five percent of prostitutes report having been victims of childhood sexual abuse.

[10] Note that many human traffickers will infiltrate support groups to find vulnerable victims.

Kat, to learn that her would-be rescuer was trying to become her online pimp.

Eventually, this gentleman decided he was done with the relationship. He left Kat and her two boys with nothing. News of this filtered back to me and Sheila, through Deidre, and we decided to offer Kat first and last month's rent, along with our church, so she could find a place to stay.

At first Kat said no. By this time, she had started to do some advocacy and frontline work with an organization dealing with human trafficking victims. We later learned that when she had been abandoned by her would-be rescuer, there was a moment when she had almost returned to prostitution. She had even made contact with an old client and gone to a hotel room, but as she sat on the bed waiting, she realized if she went through with it this time there would be no turning back and she would be lost. That's when she agreed to take the rent money.

We moved Kat to the only house in the area she could find given the fact that she was now on welfare and living well below the poverty line. The house happened to be less than five kilometres from where Sheila and I live, so we offered practical help in the form of food and gas cards to supplement her income.[11] This is where God started to prune and train me!

You can read this story and think to yourself, *What a great person Todd is, what a hero of the faith to help out a destitute ex-prostitute!* Here's the problem… I struggle with money, and all of a sudden I had another family to support. I'm not talking about a few hundred dollars here and there; we spent tens of thousands. I'd worked hard to earn money and build a nest egg to retire someday, and now that retirement seemed to be evaporating because I had a new financial responsibility I hadn't seen coming. And I fought it! Boy did I fight it. On the surface, I seemed like a hero. Underneath, I wasn't liking this one bit. There probably has never been a more unwilling hero.

But in the end, I've seen the situation for what it is. It's not my money… it's God's. That is the lesson I needed to learn. That was my

---

[11] Our church and an anonymous donor also provided some assistance.

training. I had been blessed in order to bless others. I had to loosen my grip and be guided into the right mindset by the Master Gardener.

More importantly, Kat has been such a blessing in our lives. She calls us her spiritual parents, and she's become the daughter we never had.

I tell you all this because this lesson was hard for me to learn, and it took years. I wish it had taken moments.

What hard lesson are you dealing with? Learn it fast!

At the end of the day, this whole concept of being trained and pruned, and of enjoying the process, is countercultural—not only to us North Americans, but to all mankind in general. We want things to be easy. We avoid pain because it's uncomfortable and it hurts.

But if we are to grow as Christians, we have to be countercultural. We need to embrace pain and see rebuke as the loving gesture of our Father who wants the best for us. He wants us to have life and have it abundantly, and to achieve that some pruning and training needs to take place. Receive it as joy! Acknowledge it as the loving hand of the Father. Consider it as evidence that God isn't done with you.

Know that you are still a child of the King, and remember that God only disciplines those who belong to Him. If you're being worked on... alleluia! If you ever need confirmation about this process, grab a Bible and read Hebrews 11. Read about the heroes of the faith, and then find their stories in the Old Testament. Their journeys weren't easy ones, and they had to endure trials, pruning, and training in their walks with God.

In the end, that is the point: to walk humbly with our God.

Harvest Time

1. God trains the ones He loves. Describe the last time you felt God rebuking you. How did you react? What was the consequence? How have you changed?
2. Being lukewarm means to be apathetic. How would you describe your relationship with Jesus right now? Are you on fire?

Cold? Lukewarm? What would help you fall in love with Jesus again? Do you need to start or stop doing something?

3. Consider David and the weight of his sin. What sin are you carrying in you that is crushing your bones? These are the sins you don't even want to write down in case someone sees it. Are you ready to have it pruned and removed? Confess and repent your sins to God and ask for His cleansing.

4. How trainable are you? What do you feel needs to be let go in your life?

5. Remember the tendrils I wrote about, which strive under tension. What areas of your life right now are under tension? It could be your finances, relationships, work, or health. Describe the situation. How are you clinging to Christ in the midst of this stress? If not, how can you start?

6. In terms of the unproductive areas of your life, what needs to be plucked away? What are your time-wasters? Perhaps it's Facebook, social media, TV, video games, or other forms of entertainment.

Chapter Five
Disease and Pests

There is a war going on in the vineyard! Diseases, fungi, and pests are looking to infect and feed off the vines. Some diseases attack the roots, leaves, and new shoots. Pests dine on the buds, leaves, and fruit. Larger pests, like deer, raccoons, rabbits, and mice, like to eat the tender shoots or girdle the bark off the base of the vine during harsh winters. It can be frustrating to spend a season caring for your vines and bringing your fruit to harvest only to have some marauding fat raccoon dine on your produce.

Veraison.

In August, I need to net the grape vines, because at this point the fruit has gone through a process called veraison. This is when the grapes transform from green balls and take on their deep purple colour.

I can always tell when the time is getting near, because I can see it. The bird population explodes and they get very interested in the vines and the bounty they hold. To protect the fruit, I cover them with a netting that drapes down to the ground on both sides, forming a great barrier. But it also forms a comfortable hammock for big fat raccoons to climb up to the top; they rest in the netting and use their little thief fingers to pluck grapes. I can feel my blood pressure rising just thinking about it!

The most important thing about pest management is to be diligent in walking around the vineyard and observing what's going on. Look for evidence on the leaves or in the plant for any pest activities that need to be taken care of. For instance, if in the early spring I see new buds with holes eaten out of the middle, I know I have some grape flea beetles.

If I start to see some leaves with their edges rolled under, I know I can unroll them and discover a little green worm chewing away. If I see leaves that are "skeletonized," meaning that all the green has been eaten but the vein network is left intact, that means the Japanese beetles have moved in.

Sometimes you can hold off on spraying for these pests, as natural predators will move in to feed on what's eating your grapes. But if the pest population isn't controlled naturally, sometimes you need to spray. I don't like doing this, because the sprays tend to wipe out most everything. In the grand scheme of things, there seems to be a never-ending supply of insects and bugs. All we're trying to do is control them on this little plot of land.

When it comes to disease, though, it's always best to spray before you see evidence of attack. It's easier to prevent disease than to eradicate it after it shows up. Frankly, once disease enters the vineyard, it's pretty much impossible to get it out. I usually spray lime sulphur/horticultural oil in the late winter and early spring to control overwintering pests and diseases.

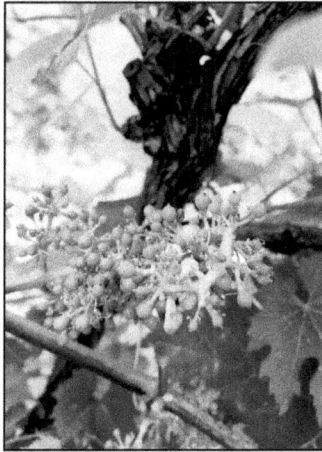

Start of powdery mildew. The battle is on!

But the majority of my battle is with powdery mildew, which can destroy a crop. As a matter of fact, I've had full seasons wiped out because of powdery mildew. I think my friends are tired of me whining and complaining about it.

The maddening aspect of this disease is that it's very hard to tell when you have an outbreak—until one day you walk out into the vineyard and it looks like someone has snuck into your vineyard overnight and sprinkled icing sugar over all your beautiful grape clusters. It sucks the wind right out of you.

I remember the first time I had a serious outbreak. I did some quick research and found an organic solution online that called for using a mixture of baking soda, light mineral oil, and water. Baking soda and water! I wasn't baking a cake here. It was like battling a rhino with a flyswatter. I sprayed and sprayed, I fought hard, and in the end I lost the majority of the crop. It was heartbreaking, to say the least.

But you'll notice that I said the *majority* of the crop.

Every year, a race takes place in the vineyard between disease and veraison. Remember the process I described earlier, where the grapes change colour? This is a glorious event, because if the grapes can get to this stage, they become immune to most diseases and can make it through to harvest. When you have a severe breakout of disease, you hope and pray for veraison to come quickly.

All this battling in the vineyard has taught me some significant lessons about God and the world in which we live.

If the vineyard is a metaphor for the world, we can see the good fruit that God is trying to grow and harvest, but disease and evil exists as well. God, the Master Gardener, is warring against the evil in the vineyard, and we, the fruit-bearing branches, are in the world being exposed to evil on a daily basis. We can't help this, but Jesus prayed for us just as He prayed for His disciples:

> After Jesus said this, he looked toward heaven and prayed: "Father, the hour has come. Glorify your Son, that your Son may glorify you. For you granted him authority over all people that he might give eternal life to all those you have given him. Now this is eternal life: that they know you, the only true God, and Jesus Christ, whom you have sent. I have brought you glory on earth by finishing the work you gave me to do. And now, Father, glorify me in your presence with the glory I had with you before the world began.
>
> "I have revealed you to those whom you gave me out of the world. They were yours; you gave them to me and they have obeyed your word. Now they know that everything you have given me comes from you. For I gave them the words you gave me and they accepted them. They knew with certainty that I came from you, and they believed that you sent me. I pray for them. I am not praying for the world, but for those you have given me, for they are yours. All I have is yours, and all you have is mine. And glory has come to me through them. I will remain in the world no longer, but they are still in the world, and I am coming to you. Holy Father, protect them by the power of your name, the name you gave me, so that they may be one as we are one. While I was with them, I protected them and kept them safe by that name

you gave me. None has been lost except the one doomed to destruction so that Scripture would be fulfilled.

"I am coming to you now, but I say these things while I am still in the world, so that they may have the full measure of my joy within them. I have given them your word and the world has hated them, for they are not of the world any more than I am of the world. My prayer is not that you take them out of the world but that you protect them from the evil one. They are not of the world, even as I am not of it. Sanctify them by the truth; your word is truth. As you sent me into the world, I have sent them into the world. For them I sanctify myself, that they too may be truly sanctified.

"My prayer is not for them alone. I pray also for those who will believe in me through their message, that all of them may be one, Father, just as you are in me and I am in you. May they also be in us so that the world may believe that you have sent me. I have given them the glory that you gave me, that they may be one as we are one—I in them and you in me—so that they may be brought to complete unity. Then the world will know that you sent me and have loved them even as you have loved me.

"Father, I want those you have given me to be with me where I am, and to see my glory, the glory you have given me because you loved me before the creation of the world.

"Righteous Father, though the world does not know you, I know you, and they know that you have sent me. I have made you known to them, and will continue to make you known in order that the love you have for me may be in them and that I myself may be in them." (John 17:1–26)

In this prayer, God recognizes that He has left us in a very sinful place, this messed-up world we live in—a vineyard that is full of disease. But God doesn't remove us from the earth upon conversion. It's not like God whisks us off to heaven when we come to faith in Jesus Christ. Why? Because there is work for us to do—like telling our neighbours about Jesus and helping the widow, the orphan, and the underprivileged. This is kingdom work. This is God's plan. We are the fruit in the vineyard who have made it to veraison. We are the remnant God has kept for His purposes on the earth to demonstrate to a lost generation grovelling in the dark that there is a good and holy God who will produce good fruit even in the midst of a diseased vineyard.

Again, the lesson resounds loud and clear: in the midst of chaos, in a world that seems to have gone mad, I can have sound peace of mind in the knowledge that God is in charge of the mess. Jesus said, *"I have told you these things, so that in me you may have peace. In this world you will have trouble. But take heart! I have overcome the world"* (John 16:33). This needs to sink into our minds and hearts. If you watch the news or hear of wars, or rumours of wars, and things don't seem fair—the rich keep getting richer, the poor keep getting abused, and children are sold into slavery—it will drive you crazy. But we can still be good fruit, close to the vine, in the vine, and make it to veraison, to the harvest! We can be Christ's hands and feet, His representatives in this messed-up vineyard called Earth.

I don't know about you, but this helps me have peace in the midst of my circumstances, in understanding the madness around me. By no means am I saying that I never waver or fear. When I watched my mother being consumed by ALS, I struggled, big-time.

But as time goes by, and your journey with the Lord deepens, your trust deepens. You find more comfort in understanding the sovereignty of God, and you trust that His ways are best.

Sometimes I don't need answers. Just like Job, who had everything but his life and his wife taken from him, said, after having God question him for four full chapters (Job 38–41),

> I know that you can do all things; no purpose of yours can be thwarted. You asked, "Who is this that obscures my plans without knowledge?" Surely I spoke of things I did not understand, things too wonderful for me to know. You said, "Listen now, and I will speak; I will question you, and you shall

answer me." My ears had heard of you but now my eyes have seen you. *Therefore I despise myself and repent in dust and ashes.* (Job 42:1–6)

Note that he said, *"Surely I spoke of things I did not understand…"* I've learned that lesson, and continue to learn that lesson, but I think I need less distance and time as I trust Him more and more.

Let me tell a story. I suffer from lower back issues, which developed over a lifetime of playing hockey and lifting weights. One of the things I bought myself in order to deal with the pain was an inversion table, a contraption in which you clamp your ankles into spring-loaded clamps. Then you put your hands over your head as the table pivots backward into various degrees of incline, anything from a slight decline to a vertical position where you're literally hanging from your ankles. This actually provided decent traction on my vertebrae and helped me overcome some bulging disc issues.

At one point, I went a long time between lower back episodes. Rather than keep using the table for regular maintenance, I stopped using it. Fast-forward to my next flare-up! I got on the table and went straight to vertical. Not smart! I gave myself a case of positional vertigo, meaning that I scrambled my inner ear, which controls your balance; it's kind of like a gyroscopic guidance system.

I didn't know I had developed this vertigo issue until I was at work one day, sitting at my desk composing an email. While sitting in my chair and taking a second to think about what I wanted to say in the message, I tilted my head back and looked up to the left. Instantaneously, the world spun off its axis. My vision blurred and I couldn't focus. The world seemed to spin at an astronomical rate. In fear, I clamped my hands down hard on the arms of my chair in an insane effort to put the brakes on the spinning. I couldn't even tell you how long the episode lasted, but finally it subsided.

I had never experienced that before, and I was freaked out of my mind trying to figure out what had just happened. Had I suffered a stroke? I ended up getting in to see my doctor, and he calmly informed me that I'd had an episode of vertigo. He said I was lucky that it had happened in my office, because for other people it sometimes happens while driving.

The doctor wrote me a prescription, and I left the office not feeling comfortable with the idea of popping pills. I went home and started doing some online research. I discovered there are different types of vertigo, one of which is positional vertigo. The home cure for positional vertigo consists of sitting on the edge of your bed with your feet planted on the floor. You are to turn your head to the left, then fling yourself over onto your right side. This sudden movement is supposed to trigger an episode. The key to the exercise is that you count off the seconds to gauge how long the episode lasts. You then lay on your right side until the spinning stops, then sit upright again, which triggers another event. You then count again, turn your head to the right, and fling yourself back on your left side. You're supposed to repeat this process at least twice per day.

Here's the reason I'm sharing this story with you. The number of seconds between episodes lessens over time as your body and inner ear adjusts. In other words, you're retraining yourself. The counting served as biofeedback to illustrate this and assure me that I was healing and that things were getting better.

Eventually I stopped counting, because the episodes stopped. And I've never had another one since.

My trust in God is kind of like that vertigo training exercise. The world seems to spin out of control, but the time between my doubt and regaining trust gets shorter and shorter. My peace and rest in a trustworthy Lord returns faster.

This lesson also helps me to understand my role as a Christian. The fact that good fruit can exist, that people dedicated to Christ can make a difference in the world, is one of the most significant proofs to a doubting world that God is real. It all comes down to one thing: changed lives. What I was before is no more. I've gone through my change, my metamorphosis, my veraison, my repentance.

The power of a changed life is one of the most significant evidences that God is still in the redemption business. These are people who can say, "I was a former (fill in the blank), but then I met Jesus and my life changed. I found life. What I was living before was nothing compared to what I am living now." This isn't a cult of a few lost and misguided people. Millions and millions of people share this story. They have believed in Jesus and had their lives changed. They now live for a God who saved and ransomed them. They now lend a hand, serve their brethren and neighbours, and help the widow and the orphan. In short, they show the love of Jesus, the love of God, to a lost world. And the world says, "Why would you do this? Why would you help me? Why do you have peace even though we have the same troubles? How can I get that peace?"

We are representatives to the world that God is still the Master Gardener, that He is still active in the vineyard, and that good fruit can grow in a disease-infested world.

The last lesson that battling disease in the vineyard has taught me has to do with the vulnerability of new growth. It always seems that the new shoots are more susceptible to disease. The older, more mature growth is a little more robust. This helps me to understand the growth and perils that face a new Christian. When we're new in faith, we may still be swayed or lose our way. The Apostle Paul saw this in the early church in Galatia and wrote,

> Paul, an apostle—sent not from men nor by a man, but by Jesus Christ and God the Father, who raised him from the dead—and all the brothers and sisters with me,
>
> To the churches in Galatia: Grace and peace to you from God our Father and the Lord Jesus Christ, who gave himself for our sins to rescue us from the present evil age, according to the will of our God and Father, to whom be glory for ever and ever. Amen.
>
> I am astonished that you are so quickly deserting the one who called you to live in the grace of Christ and are turning to a different gospel—which is really no gospel at all. Evidently some people are throwing you into confusion and are trying to pervert the gospel of Christ. But even if we or an angel from heaven should preach a gospel other than the one we

preached to you, let them be under God's curse! As we have already said, so now I say again: If anybody is preaching to you a gospel other than what you accepted, let them be under God's curse! (Galatians 1:1–9)

Paul doesn't mince words here. Those who preach a gospel other than the one preached by the apostles are to be under God's curse. That sure sounds like disease in the vineyard to me!

New Christians are vulnerable until they grow deep roots and develop into strong branches on the vine. They need to be mentored and prayed for, tended and cared for.

I saw a lot of this when Sheila and I were youth leaders. Tender shoots are so easily swayed by the doctrine of the day. But it's better to take preventive measures before disease shows up. The only thing I can advise you to do is to *be present.* That's it. Just as I walk the vineyard to constantly observe what's happening, you need to walk your proverbial vineyard, which may be your novice Christian friend's life. Be present. Don't be a pest, but be present. Take the time to observe, train, correct, love, encourage, and build up. As a mentor, you're a gardener, too!

That last lesson is one I take from my good friend Kat, the executive director of our charity, Rising Angels. Although a former prostitute, she has become a born-again Christian. The mission of Rising Angels is to bring sex trade education to professionals and the public, and to provide supportive services and safe environments to women exploited by the sex trade, allowing them to experience physical, mental, social, and spiritual restoration in their lives.

We offer several types of help, including peer mentoring and life coaching, crisis intervention and trauma-informed care, rent assistance, transportation to and from appointments, rehab support, and help with food, personal hygiene, and clothing.

Our short-term mandate is to provide survivor-led mentoring and trauma-informed care. We meet people's basic needs, and provide advocacy and education, creating awareness and understanding among professionals, law enforcement, schools, churches, and other interest groups. Our long-term mandate is to build a series of transitional complexes which will house ten to twenty people at a time. In these homes, we will be able to offer extended stays and support for up to two years. We can also help provide education and job skills training and assist people in finding work placements. These complexes will be fully staffed with psychologists and life coaches to help people grow and develop their spiritual lives.[12]

I mention all this because I've had my eyes opened regarding prostitution. Did you know that the average age of entry is fourteen? They are babies being preyed on by wolves, and they can be preyed upon because they're vulnerable. Why are they vulnerable? Because most of these children have experienced some kind of abuse as children. It's not necessarily sexual abuse; it can be physical or psychological. But these people are broken, damaged, and looking for love. Katarina, during her many years of dealing with the heartbroken parents of victims, now tells any parent who will listen to get nosy and look for the signs of a child who is being groomed in prostitution.

Parents, protect your children. Get nosy. Get involved. Be present!

Harvest Time

1. Describe how you are seeing the veraison change in your own life. This is the process of becoming something else, of becoming immune or safe in an evil world, set apart and reserved for good works. What current kingdom work are you involved with?

2. How easy is it for you to trust God in all your circumstances? Why? What are you trusting God with right now? What gives you spiritual vertigo? In other words, what's scrambling your balance with God? The biofeedback exercise helps us to feel the presence of the Lord and shorten the length of time that passes between the onset of doubt and the return of trust.

3. Write out a list of the times when God has shown up in your life. Let's call these spiritual landmarks. This should be a list of all the times when you were able to claim the goodness of God, or

---

[12] For further information about Rising Angels, visit www.risingangels.net.

when you knew He had shown up for you. These are causes for trust, and trust leads to confidence. After you make your list, continue to add to it on a daily basis until you know that you know that you know that God is good.

4. A changed life—in other words, our stories and testimonies—is powerful evidence that God is still at work in the vineyard. Write out your story. What are you ready to share about your story of change? I challenge you to go share it with someone... today!

Chapter Six
Canopy Management

After the growing season has started and the vines are in full growth mode, one of my major jobs is canopy management. The canopy refers to the leaves and branches that flourish in the vineyard. You can see from the pictures below what it looks like at the start of spring and what it looks like around end of June.

Vines after pruning in late April 2018.

Vigorous vine growth at mid-June.

Misguided growth in need of training.

The vines are amazingly prolific, and left to their own devices, without any supervision or intervention, they pump out a ridiculous amount of growth. Some new branches will grow twenty feet or more if you let them. Sometimes the growth is so heavy, you can't see the forest for the trees, so to speak. Some vines get away from you and grow out to amazing lengths, undetected.

I try not to let this happen too often, because I want to control the canopy growth. Why? There are a few key reasons.

Keeping the canopy growth in check, appropriately thinned, allows space around the leaves and fruit. This space is critical when it comes to disease management.

One of the things that promotes disease faster than anything else is moisture. Water and dew provide a superhighway for some of these little tail-whipping organisms to move around and climb on the vines. To block access, one of the best things you can do is to thin out the canopy and ensure that leaves, branches, and fruit have a lot of space around them to promote good drying.

This thinning process includes stripping certain leaves so they aren't blocking the fruit from sunlight. This practice alone, learned painfully slow over the years, has really helped to up my game when it comes to the total harvest yield and yield quality.

Let's stop and talk numbers for a moment. My little vineyard has about one hundred fifty vines, and from that I will take in about four hundred fifty pounds of fruit, about three pounds of fruit per vine. That may not sound like much, but we can get approximately one bottle of wine per vine. As the farmer, I get half, and Klaus, my partner and the brains behind the operation, gets the other half.

I'm most pleased with the Brix content of the grapes. Brix is a measurement of sugar concentration. A Brix refractor is basically a prism on which you drop some grape or fruit juice and hold it up to a light source to peer through. A grid on the glass plate within the prism refracts the light through the juice to provide a Brix reading of the sugar content of the juice. The Brix readings I've been able to achieve over the last two years have been 22.2 (in 2016), and 22.0 (in 2017). Klaus gave me great encouragement, filling me with pride, to note that my Brix numbers and fruit quality exceed that which comes from the commercial producers in the Niagara Falls growing area. Given my more northern location, in a harsher environment, I'm very happy to be able to produce such high quality.

Remember, the best wine is made where the grapes are the most stressed!

Thinning the vines is a constant grooming process during which I walk the vineyard with my trusty pruning shears in hand and twine in my pocket. After years of stupidity—again, I'm not the quickest student—I've learned not to walk into the vineyard without taking my shears and some twine. If I forget, it's guaranteed that I'll find something that needs taking care of, and then I'll have to hike all the way back to the garage to get the shears and twine. It's better to have them with me and not need them.

I'll often bring my trusty wheelbarrow, too. Why, you ask? Because rather than throw the cuttings onto the ground to compost, I'll take them to a pile far from the vineyard to eventually burn after they've dried out somewhat. I do this for the purpose of disease management. I don't want to take any chances that disease exists in the cuttings. By throwing them on the ground, I'd just be reintroducing that disease to the vines and reinfect the plant. Not smart.

On these walks, I look for growth that's crowding and touching, which only serves to trap moisture and delay the drying process. I also look to strip away leaves that cover up the grape clusters so they can hang in the open and dangle in the wind.

It's also critical to position the fruit. Commercial vineyards will use what's called a double wire setup in which the vine is pruned to have two lower arms; the growth is then forced between two wires so that the fruit hangs low and the canopy grows up between the wires.[13] This ensures that the fruit is free and clear to hang in the sun and air out. It also ensures that any spraying will be sure to fully cover the plant. It's handy for the harvest, too, because a machine can go up and down the rows and pull the low-hanging fruit very easily.

It's amazing to watch the canopy management in a commercial vineyard because they have special hedging machines that basically mow the growth that leans into the row space versus growing up between the wires. It's certainly not as caring and hands-on as my operation! I use a four-cane Knifkin system which is a little more wild and random and can be a handful if you don't stay on top of it. Your fruit can grow on any one of three wires, so it's important to strip the leaves and make sure the fruit hangs out in the open to receive sunlight and air.

The other necessity is to limit the growth itself so that the branch puts more of its effort into grape production and quality versus pumping out extra feet of vine that will serve no purpose except to sap strength from fruit production. Too much growth will end up crowding out a neighbouring vine's efforts, and that growth is only going to end up getting cut away the next year anyhow.

Managing growth also has a lot to do with removing lateral branches. These are the branches that grow out of the leaf crotches, where the leaf stem meets the branch. I want to remove these, as they won't serve a purpose next year, and they only sap energy and create unwanted shade this year. Get 'em outta here! The branch needs to get adequate sunlight, because it's doing two things at once: growing fruit for this year's harvest and growing buds that will become new growth next year.

---

[13] Perhaps this is where the term "low-hanging fruit" comes from.

Start of lateral growth and unwanted shade.

This planning involves tending to new branches and looking to see if there are new branches that may not have fruit on them this year but would be in really nice positions for next year. You have to be like a great chess player, always thinking multiple moves ahead.

When I wander the vineyard, snipping, cutting, tying, and stripping leaves, I have time to meditate on how God continues to work with me and on me. I've grown more accustomed to the guiding hand of the Father. In the earlier days of my Christian walk, I'd say I wasn't the easiest child to discipline. Like many of you, I found there were certain things in my life that were easier to give up than others. The problem was those areas where I didn't necessarily trust Jesus to get into, like my finances.

I always wanted to make money and save it in an effort to build up a war chest of dollars and cents that would insulate me from the waves and storms of life. I wanted to have the kind of money that would let me say "Great" if my boss walked in and told me I was being let go. Sheila and I have worked hard. We've been frugal and ended up paying off our mortgage eight years ago. We've been diligent about putting money away into retirement savings accounts and investments.

But as time has gone by, and as God has continued to work on my canopy, trimming away certain things from my life, He has made it apparent that He has blessed me so that I can be a blessing to others, loosening my hand and wallet more often. The bottom line is that it's not my money anyway. I'm nothing more than a steward of God's blessings.

This makes me think of the parable Jesus told about the bags of gold:

> Again, it will be like a man going on a journey, who called his servants and entrusted his wealth to them. To one he gave five bags of gold, to another two bags, and to another one bag, each according to his ability. Then he went on his journey. The man who had received five bags of gold went at once and put his money to work and gained five bags more. So also, the one with two bags of gold gained two more. But the man who had received one bag went off, dug a hole in the ground and hid his master's money.
>
> After a long time the master of those servants returned and settled accounts with them. The man who had received five bags of gold brought the other five. "Master," he said, "you entrusted me with five bags of gold. See, I have gained five more."
>
> His master replied, "Well done, good and faithful servant! You have been faithful with a few things; I will put you in charge of many things. Come and share your master's happiness!"
>
> The man with two bags of gold also came. "Master," he said, "you entrusted me with two bags of gold; see, I have gained two more."
>
> His master replied, "Well done, good and faithful servant! You have been faithful with a few things; I will put you in charge of many things. Come and share your master's happiness!"
>
> Then the man who had received one bag of gold came. "Master," he said, "I knew that you are a hard man, harvesting where you have not sown and gathering where you have not scattered seed. So I was afraid and went out and hid your gold in the ground. See, here is what belongs to you."
>
> His master replied, "You wicked, lazy servant! So you knew that I harvest where I have not sown and gather where I

have not scattered seed? Well then, you should have put my money on deposit with the bankers, so that when I returned I would have received it back with interest.

"So take the bag of gold from him and give it to the one who has ten bags. For whoever has will be given more, and they will have an abundance. Whoever does not have, even what they have will be taken from them. And throw that worthless servant outside, into the darkness, where there will be weeping and gnashing of teeth." (Matthew 25:14–30)

We've been blessed with much, and to close our hand around it, to not invest it in kingdom work, makes us wicked, lazy servants. My former way of thinking put me squarely in that category.

But as my journey carried on and my understanding of money and finances took on a spiritual context, I was able to recognize that I needed to open this area of my life to Jesus—as well as all the other areas.

I know it's a fairly worn Christian metaphor, but I'll tread on it some more. Your life is like a house, and each room is like an area of your life. The kitchen, for example, could represent food and health, the bedroom could represent your sexuality, the bathroom... well, let's not go there. But you get the picture.

There are certain rooms I have no issue letting Jesus into, but what about the room that has my money issues in it? I wanted to keep that door closed. That was my business!

Many of you may be familiar with the painting that depicts Jesus standing at a door and knocking. In the image, there's no doorknob on Jesus's side of the door, meaning that He won't just let Himself into your life. You need to open the door from your side.

In my case, He knocked and knocked and knocked.

Eventually, the door opened a crack. I opened my wallet and gave. And here's the crazy part: when I give, I find that I still have enough left over to save for the life I'm looking for. Sheila and I are in a good spot. Retirement is on the horizon at a young enough age that we can travel and do all the things we hope to enjoy together in our twilight years. Do I own a BMW or a Mercedes? No, but that was never for me. I couldn't have brought myself to own something that would depreciate so substantially the minute I drove it off the lot. I have never been driven to impress people with the cars I drove or the watches on my wrist. I live in a pretty big house—did I mention it's drafty?—with lots of land, and I still do all my own yardwork.

A boss once said to me, "Why do you waste time mowing your lawn and doing yardwork? Just make another big sale and hire someone to do it!" Again, that's not me. I still enjoy winning the new customer and making the big sale, but it's more so that I can use the money to help my church, help with missions, and help our friend Kat make it out of prostitution. You see, I've learned not to bury wealth and hoard it for myself. I want to invest it in God's economy.

From a different perspective, what if I had kept all my money and never given all those thousands of dollars back to God? I probably could have retired five years ago, but I would have been so much poorer. Remember what Jesus said:

> Do not store up for yourselves treasures on earth, where moths and vermin destroy, and where thieves break in and steal. But store up for yourselves treasures in heaven, where moths and vermin do not destroy, and where thieves do not break in and steal. For where your treasure is, there your heart will be also.
>
> The eye is the lamp of the body. If your eyes are healthy, your whole body will be full of light. But if your eyes are unhealthy, your whole body will be full of darkness. If then the light within you is darkness, how great is that darkness!
>
> No one can serve two masters. Either you will hate the one and love the other, or you will be devoted to the one and despise the other. You cannot serve both God and money. (Matthew 6:19–24)

It's so true! I want to invest in God's work, to play a part on God's Wall Street.

Do I regret giving or miss the money? I can't lie to you and say it has always been easy, but it's getting easier. I can see the good work the money does, and I'm not living on the streets. It's a win-win as far as I can see.

Doing the work we do at Rising Angels has been a blessing to me. Through it, I get to meet so many like-minded Christians who share the same perspective. God provides divine appointments for us to meet with groups and speak about human trafficking, and He then nudges people to give to the cause. We see it time and time again. People who have a heart for God's work open their wallets and hearts and literally save women with their donations.[14]

Canopy management also helps me understand how God removes distractions and obstacles from my walk with Him.

In the parable of the sower, Jesus talks about a farmer (representing Jesus) who went out to sow some seed (representing the good news of the gospel). Some of that seed (representing the message from heaven) fell on a path and was snatched away by someone (representing Satan and his demons). Other seed fell on stony ground, and although it could take root it died shortly after because its roots were short—in other words, it wasn't grounded in faith. Some seed fell amongst weeds and was choked out because of the worries and distractions of life.

But some of the seed fell on good and receptive ground, meaning that the gospel was heard by those who were ready to hear it. In those circumstances, the seed produced a crop a hundred times larger than what had originally been sown!

That same day Jesus went out of the house and sat by the lake. Such large crowds gathered around him that he got into a boat and sat in it, while all the people stood on the shore. Then he told them many things in parables, saying: "A farmer went out to sow his seed. As he was scattering the seed, some fell along the path, and the birds came and ate

---

[14] Right now, we're longing and praying for someone with lots of real estate to contact us to donate land and facilities for our planned transition home. You know who you are! Contact us at www.risingangels.net.

it up. Some fell on rocky places, where it did not have much soil. It sprang up quickly, because the soil was shallow. But when the sun came up, the plants were scorched, and they withered because they had no root. Other seed fell among thorns, which grew up and choked the plants. Still other seed fell on good soil, where it produced a crop—a hundred, sixty or thirty times what was sown. Whoever has ears, let them hear."

The disciples came to him and asked, "Why do you speak to the people in parables?"

He replied, "Because the knowledge of the secrets of the kingdom of heaven has been given to you, but not to them. Whoever has will be given more, and they will have an abundance. Whoever does not have, even what they have will be taken from them. This is why I speak to them in parables: 'Though seeing, they do not see; though hearing, they do not hear or understand.'" (Matthew 13:1–13)

God's canopy management in my life removes distractions, helping me to hear and respond to God's call. Worries, concerns, selfishness, idleness, laziness... all of these can be weeds in my life that crowd out God's voice. God's pruning hand shows me areas where I'm being distracted in unhealthy ways and wasting my time, failing to invest in God's economy. I'm thankful for His continued grooming and guidance, giving me direction.

I appreciate learning these lessons from the vines because they help me see the harsh reality of an overfruiting branch. A branch that's left to bear too much fruit will cause burnout and fatigue in that branch. If it tries to support too much growth, next year it will be barren because it will have wasted itself.

That's the danger we can run into if we don't measure and monitor what we get involved in. I've seen Christians who sit on multiple committees, serve on boards, and volunteer like crazy... and after a while they burn out. Should we serve? Yes. Destroy ourselves? No. We're of no use to God if we take on too much.

If you're asking yourself why you've taken on a particular project and your answer is "Because I'm the only one qualified" or "Because no one else would," then check your motive. You shouldn't be feeling a guilt trip, or pride.

A calling from God will equip you to do the task, and it will be confirmed by the church and your fellow Christians. You'll be uplifted by holy power to do the job. If you're feeling burned out, or if you lack enthusiasm for kingdom work, perhaps take a step back to see where some grooming and pruning might be needed.

It's important to remain open and flexible to the guiding hand of the Master Gardener. Remain open and flexible to new direction and teaching, and hold loosely to the things in your life that may need to be stripped away.

Harvest Time

1. Take a walk down memory lane and think about your walk with Christ. What was easy to change in the early days? What areas have you not let God into? What "room" in your life is off-limits to the Lord? Be honest. Does He have free rein everywhere?

2. Consider the parable of the bags of gold. Which of the servants in the parable do you identify with and why? How are you actively growing the investment Jesus has made in you? Remember that you were bought for a price.

3. What is your attitude about money? Describe your heavenly understanding about money. Write it down, and then read it! Does what you wrote align with the way you actually live?

4. As far as canopy management goes, what distractions exist in your life? Are they crowding out your relationship with Christ? Are you like the receptive soil in the parable of the sower and the seed? How have you remained flexible and open to new direction and thinking?

Chapter Seven
Vines and Branches

I'd like to spend some more time talking about vines and branches, because this is one of the key illustrations in Jesus's final lesson:

> I am the true vine, and my Father is the gardener. He cuts off every branch in me that bears no fruit, while every branch that does bear fruit he prunes so that it will be even more fruitful. You are already clean because of the word I have spoken to you. Remain in me, as I also remain in you. No branch can bear fruit by itself; it must remain in the vine. Neither can you bear fruit unless you remain in me.
>
> I am the vine; you are the branches. If you remain in me and I in you, you will bear much fruit; apart from me you can do nothing. If you do not remain in me, you are like a branch that is thrown away and withers; such branches are picked up, thrown into the fire and burned. If you remain in me and my words remain in you, ask whatever you wish, and it will be done for you. This is to my Father's glory, that you bear much fruit, showing yourselves to be my disciples. (John 15:1–8)

The part that always stuck out to me was the phrase "*you are like a branch that is thrown away and withers.*" If you've never seen a new branch that's been cut off the vine, it withers almost immediately.

In the following images, you can see how quickly the branch, once separated, wilts and dies. Witnessing this time and time again in the vineyard has really driven home the point about staying connected to Jesus, the true vine, and what it looks like when we're not connected.

Newly cut branch.

Same branch wilting after ten minutes of separation from the vine.

Again, Jesus is a master storyteller. His audience, the disciples, would surely have understood this imagery because they would have seen branches being cut from vine, then gathered for the fire. Wine and vineyards were such an important part of their society and culture. Many of them kept vines to provide wines for their own families.

In Paul's writing to Timothy, he gives the young man some fatherly advice, saying, "*Stop drinking only water, and use a little wine because of your stomach and your frequent illnesses*" (1 Timothy 5:23).

This leads me to think that wine and grapes were so engrained in the culture of the day that the image Jesus used would have been a vivid one.

New growth has a very weak connection to the vine. I can easily rub out new unwanted buds, and at times I've accidentally caused a bud to be flicked off by simply brushing up against a plant. You need to move around the plant carefully in the spring so as not to lose something you really wanted.

This weak connection exists for the first month or so, until the new growth has had time to deeply connect to the main vine. The connection point then fuses and becomes inseparable. To break off the branch, you'd need to snap the junction point.

This makes me think of our journey as Christians. In the beginning, our connection point to the vine (Jesus) is so tenuous and delicate that it needs to be nurtured. The root isn't deep, so there's a risk of new Christians being disconnected. As mature Christians, we need to nurture new Christians to deepen their connection to the vine. It's their own journey and we can't make the connection for them, but we can mentor them, encouraging them to be in the Word.

Solid mentoring programs should be a critical part of every church's mandate. We seem to be anxious to see conversions, but as soon as a new Christian accepts the Lord we kind of abandon that project and move on to the next thing. But we need to really think about how we tend this new growth. At conversion, the Holy Spirit comes to dwell within new believers, and the Spirit will guide and instruct them, but the body of believers has a role to play in terms of building up and encouraging them.

In the early days of my conversion, I had a fire in my soul, but this period also came with a lot of confusion. I would go to church and hear older, grizzled Christians say things like, "I heard a word from the Lord!"

Oh my gosh, I'd think to myself. *Does that person really audibly hear the voice of God? Is it a booming voice? Thunderously deep? Or is it a gentle, lilting voice?*

I'd never heard from the Lord! Was I really a Christian? Had that whole conversion thing really happened? Was I saved?

Maybe you've experienced, or are experiencing, the same. If so, I'm here to tell those of you who represent the mature Christian crowd, knock it off with the Christianese! Some of the phrases we use can be so damaging to uneducated new believers. We need to ensure they understand what we're talking about.[15]

It wasn't until our church put on a fantastic study called "Experiencing God: Knowing and Hearing the Voice of God," by Henry Blackaby, that I finally learned what hearing the voice of God actually meant. I learned that many people don't hear an audible voice; they hear God speaking through the reading of the Bible, through other Christians, through prayer, and through sermon messages. I discovered that I hear God's voice through repetitive messages that seem to come at me from various, unrelated sources. They indicate to me that God is trying to get my attention about something.

Let me share how this has actually played out for me. Four years into my Christian journey, I wasn't really serving in the church, but I certainly felt a conviction that I needed to get involved. I could see that the Bible called for people to serve.

On my drive to work one morning, I was listening to a Christian radio station and heard Chuck Swindoll, one of my favourite speakers, give a message about serving in the church. One of his statements caught me square in the chin: "You gotta get off the bench and into the game!" I come from a sports background, so that statement really resonated with me.

Later on, when speaking to a friend and elder, he asked me if I'd ever thought of getting involved with the senior youth. That sounded a lot like a serving opportunity, an invitation to get off the bench. When I got home that day, Sheila told me that she had been thinking about getting involved with the youth group. There you go!

This is a perfect example of how I hear the voice of God. The Spirit was already pressing in on me through my Bible study. Then I heard a confirming message on the radio. Then a fellow Christian spoke to

---

[15] Some examples of Christianese: "When God closes a door, He opens a window," "You're never more safe than when you're in God's will," "Let go and let God," "God will never give you more than you can handle," "Everything happens for a reason," "God needed another angel," "Love the sinner; hate the sin," "Do life together," "Just pray harder," or "It's just the way God made me."

me about the same topic. Finally, my wife had been having the same thoughts. All these things were disconnected yet related. That's how God grabs my attention.

Other times, I'll be reading my Bible only to get in my car and hear the exact same message on the radio, even using the same scriptures. Then I'll go to church on Sunday only to hear my pastor preach on the same verse!

Okay, God, I'll pray. I get it. You want me to take a real good look at these verses and see what you're speaking to me!

Call it coincidence if you want, but to me this is the voice of God.

Your experience of hearing God may be totally different. Hey, we can't all have burning bush experiences like Moses! But this illustrates my point about new Christians needing guidance and encouragement so as not to lose their fire, or their way, and ultimately be disconnected from the vine.

While we're on this topic of vines and branches, let me mention bull canes. What's a bull cane? It's a rogue cane that sprouts from the vine and takes off like wildfire. They're mammoth in diameter and unparalleled in growth. They shoot for the top wire and, left unchecked, will sap a lot of the energy from your plant. Here's the thing: they produce no fruit, at least not in year one. I'm always on the lookout for these rogue, braggadocio canes. They're impressive, no doubt, but they add nothing. As the tough-love vinekeeper I am, I cut them off so as not to affect the other, fruit-producing branches. These bull canes sap energy, create excess canopy growth, crowd out sunlight, and create excess density that limits air flow.

When I think of bull canes and what they represent, I better understand what Jesus was talking about when He taught about prayer and admonishing the attitude of the Pharisees:

Be careful not to practice your righteousness in front of others to be seen by them. If you do, you will have no reward from your Father in heaven.

So when you give to the needy, do not announce it with trumpets, as the hypocrites do in the synagogues and on the streets, to be honored by others. *Truly I tell you, they have received their reward in full. But when you give to the needy, do not let your left hand know what your right hand is doing, so that your giving may be in secret. Then your Father, who sees what is done in secret, will reward you.*

And when you pray, do not be like the hypocrites, for they love to pray standing in the synagogues and on the street corners to be seen by others. Truly I tell you, they have received their reward in full. But when you pray, go into your room, close the door and pray to your Father, who is unseen. Then your Father, who sees what is done in secret, will reward you. And when you pray, do not keep on babbling like pagans, for they think they will be heard because of their many words. Do not be like them, for your Father knows what you need before you ask him.

This, then, is how you should pray: "Our Father in heaven, hallowed be your name, your kingdom come, your will be done, on earth as it is in heaven. Give us today our daily bread. And forgive us our debts, as we also have forgiven our debtors. And lead us not into temptation, but deliver us from the evil one."

For if you forgive other people when they sin against you, your heavenly Father will also forgive you. But if you do not forgive others their sins, your Father will not forgive your sins. (Matthew 6:1–15)

When I look at a bull cane and see its flashiness and unproductive growth, I think about what Jesus said about not drawing attention to ourselves, and doing good deeds in secret so as not to try gaining the approval of men but rather the reward of our Father in heaven. I've known some bull canes in my life... and you probably have, too—people who give to the needy with a condition of acknowledgement, to be recognized and applauded by men. Don't do it! The moment you do, you will erase the reward of your Father in heaven.

Check your motive at the door. Are you giving to be seen, or because you have a deep understanding of the debt you owe the Lord for His love and sacrifice? You should want to use your God-given blessings to join Him in the kingdom work He has called us to.

Back when Sheila and I were first starting to work with Kat on building Rising Angels, we organized an event at our church so people could come and hear her story of childhood rape and abuse, entrapment in prostitution, and ultimate redemption. That evening, we opened people's hearts and minds to the fact that prostitution isn't a choice, that it is indeed human trafficking. Prostitution is about one person usurping power over another human being by selling that person for abuse at the hands of another. Prostitution is paid rape!

After that evening, a gentleman approached me and Sheila and said that he wanted to help. We'd known this gentleman for a number of years and knew him to be a strong, solid Christian as well as an astute businessman. He wanted to provide monthly support to Kat, which he did. The money went to Sheila, who used it for groceries and clothing for Kat and her children when in need. The only condition was that he didn't want Kat to know the support was coming from him, and to this day we have honoured that request, and Kat still has no idea who this secret benefactor was. But I'll tell you who does know— God. And He has blessed that man. It would have been easy for him to want to be known and praised as a generous and benevolent hero of the faith.

But I'll tell you why this was a great experience for Kat in her growth and maturity as a new Christian. Sheila and I were able to have a teaching moment with her. We were able to open her eyes to the fact that it wasn't a man taking care of her, but God Himself. We explained that God had called this wealthy man to faith in Jesus Christ, and this man, in following his faith, had given not out of a need to be worshiped or acknowledged but to honour his Lord Jesus Christ, who had saved him by dying on the cross and paying his penalty of sin. We all owe a great debt to our Saviour, a debt that can never be repaid. We can now use our God-given resources to do God's kingdom work here on earth.

In essence, because this man's heart was changed, and because he knew he had been called to kingdom work, he gave money to support a woman who had been a victim of injustice.

Let's do the math:

The sin of man = death
Jesus's death = man's sin

As you can see, Jesus has cancelled out death! Here's some more math:

Jesus pays for man's sin + grateful believer = cheerful giver
Cheerful giver + kingdom work = God's care for the needy

Math doesn't lie! God provided for Kat through the cheerful giver.

Let me tell you why this is so important, especially for someone like Kat. Kat has been abused by men her whole life. How trusting do you think she is going to be in a male God figure? Not very. But at the same time, Kat has also spent her life being taken care of by men. Pimps have the money. Johns have the money. They control the purse strings. In Kat's world, money came from men... men who wanted to abuse her sexually. So if you want to survive in Kat's world, you need to entice a man to desire you so that you'll be taken care of. Prostitutes don't want to have sex with strangers... they want to survive!

But now came a strange situation where a man wanted to give her money to survive, but he didn't want sex from her. He just wanted to follow the commands of his Saviour. From this, Kat learned that maybe there are some male figures out there who can be trusted. Above all, she became certain that God could be trusted, because He had shown up to take care of her.

I told Kat that God was going to show her that He was the one she needed to rely on. She wouldn't have to flirt with men anymore or try to entice them to get what she wanted. God Himself would provide. And He has! Big-time.

As I mentioned before, Kat is now the executive director of Rising Angels. She has a board of directors and a full-time job that pays well and provides benefits. God did that for her! Sure, human beings had to provide the means by which the resources became available to get things up and running, but it was God who mobilized their hearts. It's a brilliant story when you think about it. God is still in business. He's still taking the five loaves and two fishes and multiplying it to feed thousands. The question is simple. What do you have in your hands? How has God blessed you? How can you help a survivor?

Remember that Jesus said,

> I am the vine; you are the branches. If you remain in me and I in you, you will bear much fruit; apart from me you can do nothing. If you do not remain in me, you are like a branch that is thrown away and withers; such branches are picked up, thrown into the fire and burned. If you remain in me and my words remain in you, ask whatever you wish, and it will be done for you. This is to my Father's glory, that you bear much fruit, showing yourselves to be my disciples. (John 15:5–8)

It's so clear, isn't it? For us to bear kingdom fruit we must remain in Christ, because apart from Him we can do nothing. And the fruit we bear honours and glorifies the Father, and through it the world gains a vision of the Father. Your fruit, what you do in secret to honour God, has the cumulative effect of bringing the Father's glory to a lost and dark world that desperately needs to see that the hand of God is active, moving, and alive!

Harvest Time

1. In this chapter, I shared the way in which I hear the voice of God in my life, and typically it's through multiple sources. Describe how God speaks to you. How do you confirm that this is God and not your own thoughts?

2. Consider bull canes and the Pharisees—yes, they still exist in our churches today. How would you lovingly approach a person like this in your circle of influence and guide them towards becoming kingdom fruit-bearers?

3. Think about the last time you gave financial support. Was there a part of you that wanted recognition? What would protect your heart from that?

4. God's care comes through His fruitful believers. Is this a new concept for you? Describe a time when you were on the receiving end of a gift from a believer. How did it make you feel? Describe a time when you were the giver. How did that make you feel? Did you feel like you had really given away more than you had received?

Chapter Eight

Rain Falls on the Good and the Bad

In the design of the vineyard, it's helpful to leave a three-foot growing area between the vines. This limits the competition between the vines for resources and nutrients.

But one of the biggest battles I fight year in and year out is not only with powdery mildew and disease, but also with weeds. Weeds are aggressive and insidious. They grow in all sorts of environments. Cold weather varieties emerge in the early spring and there are those that prefer the dry heat of the dog days of summer. Whether it's cold, wet, hot, or dry, there's a weed variety looking to take up residence in your nicely tilled and manicured vineyard.

Constant vigilance is required to battle the never-ending supply of weeds, and woe be to the man or woman who leaves them to mature and go to seed. There is an old saying that goes, "One year to seed; seven to weed!" No truer words have ever been spoken.

Weeds that are allowed to go to seed in the garden or vineyard will invade your patch of paradise before you know it. And they'll keep coming back, year after year after year. I've broken my back trying to hoe, till, and harrow the rows, but when you're looking at seven rows, each approximately a hundred feet long, well... that's a mighty long row to hoe! Desperate times call for desperate measures. I'm not too proud to tell you that I've resorted to chemical means to keep them in check.

Over the last few years, I've begun using mulch as a way to keep the weeds down. You see, an act of divine intervention happened after an intense ice storm on December 22, 2013. The date is still seared into my memory. Weather warnings had indicated a large rain system moving up towards Canada from the Gulf of Mexico. When that intense rain met with some Canadian cold, it was a perfect recipe for disaster.

I remember going to bed that night naively thinking, *How bad could it be?* The answer was really bad!

That night, as the rain continued to fall, we started to hear booming sounds from outside. Each boom was then followed by a sound reminiscent of shattering glass.

How odd, I thought, nestled in my warm bed, *I guess that's the ice falling out of the trees.*

No, my dear friends. That was the sound of ice falling from the trees and taking down entire branches with it.

Somewhere during the night, when I realized that branches might be falling, I remembered that my car shelter was situated right under a large, sprawling Manitoba Maple. Oh no! My car was going to be crushed for sure.

By morning, our homestead looked like a war zone. I gritted my teeth, looked outside, and saw that the maple had indeed succumbed to the weight of ice accumulated on its limbs. Yes, huge limbs had snapped off the tree. But, miracle of miracles, the limbs had fallen all around the car shelter without hitting the car directly.

Sheila and I sprang into action.[16] I sparked up my trusty chainsaw and started hacking and slashing to liberate the car. Sheila, being

---

[16] We're a good team that way. If you and I ever meet in person, ask me what happened after a contractor punctured the water pipe in our upstairs bedroom with a floor sander.

a robust farmgirl, dragged huge branches out of the way as fast as I could cut them. We were packin' and stackin' that ice-encrusted timber as fast as we could.

It was no wonder the trees were breaking. On some of the branches, the ice was an inch thick or more. The weight of it was incredible.

Once we had freed the car, it was time to walk down the lane of misery to assess the rest of the damage.

Literally, our property looked like old black-and-white photos of World War I battlefields. The pine trees had done okay, because they were so springy. The harder woods, like sugar maples, elms, and chestnuts, sustained quite a bit of damage. The trees that got it the worst were the softwoods, the poplars and willows. They were devastated. It looked like a giant had grabbed the trees and run his hand up the trunk, stripping all the branches. The branches were everywhere. Many crossed the laneway, meaning we needed to drag them away so we could get in and out of the property.

While we were out there dragging branches, the devastation continued. The trees were still so heavy with ice. It was spooky and awe-inspiring at the same time. It would be really quiet and then, off in the distance, we'd hear a *boom!* followed by the sound of wood crashing to the ground.

"Look," I said to Sheila. "If you hear a boom, you gotta run out into the open."

As we were working, we heard a boom right near us and I yelled for her to run.

"I don't know where to run!" she yelled back, in a panic.

I looked over my shoulder to see her kind of dancing in spot like she had to pee! I grabbed her and we ran to safety.

Hindsight being twenty-twenty, we probably shouldn't have been out there. We should have stayed in the house where it was safe. But we'd kind of gotten into a damage control headspace and wanted to try fixing things right away.

We were without electricity for two days. Others in the area were without electricity for over a week. In December. At Christmas.

I had to go to a hardware store to get my barbecue's propane tanks refilled so we could cook and boil water. While standing in line, I got to talking with an East Indian gentleman who was ahead of me. We spoke about the storm, and he explained that he was getting his propane tank filled so he could bring the barbecue into the house and use it as a source of heat. Oh dear God! This sparked the ears of everyone around, who quickly told him why he shouldn't do that. Later, we heard reports that some people did die of carbon monoxide poisoning from doing this. Tragic.

We still had a huge clean-up job in front of us, so we hired a tree service to remove a number of tree limbs that had cracked and mulch the tons and tons of wood on the ground. This was back in 2013, and I still have mulch piles left today.

To make a long story short, I used that mulch on the vine rows to act as a weed barrier. It only took me eight years of vinekeeping and one environmental disaster to figure that out. Sometimes I'm not the sharpest knife in the drawer!

In His lesson, Jesus described His Father as the Gardener, or vinekeeper, who goes throughout the vineyard pruning the vines to produce fruit. Well, one of the realities of a vineyard is dealing with weeds. Weeds are the enemy of fruit, and they represent evil in the world. They are encroachers and thieves.

Yet as the Bible tells us, God causes the life-sustaining rain to fall on the good and the bad. When I live my reality in the vineyard and contemplate the existence of evil in the world, I am able to better understand what Jesus was saying in His parable of the weeds.

The kingdom of heaven is like a man who sowed good seed in his field. But while everyone was sleeping, his enemy came and sowed weeds among the wheat, and went away. When the wheat sprouted and formed heads, then the weeds also appeared.

The owner's servants came to him and said, "Sir, didn't you sow good seed in your field? Where then did the weeds come from?"

"An enemy did this," he replied.

The servants asked him, "Do you want us to go and pull them up?"

"No," he answered, "because while you are pulling the weeds, you may uproot the wheat with them. Let both grow together until the harvest. At that time I will tell the harvesters: First collect the weeds and tie them in bundles to be burned; then gather the wheat and bring it into my barn." (Matthew 13:24–30)

God sowed good seed with the best of intentions, to produce a good crop. A paradise. But an enemy came along, Satan, and sowed weeds (representing evil) amongst the goodness sown by the Father. As God's creation began to form and His goodness emerged, so did evil. We can see from Genesis that it wasn't long before Adam and Eve showed pride and Cain killed his brother Abel. Weeds!

So tell us something we don't know, Todd, you may be thinking.

Okay. The interesting part of this, to me, is that God says to the workers, "No, don't go into the world and pull out the weeds, because in doing so you might damage the good that is trying to grow. Let them both grow and come to maturity. Then they will be clearly seen for what they are."

When it's harvest time, these workers—angels, I'm sure—receive instructions to go out and gather all the weeds, all the evil and that which isn't producing what the Father intended. They are told to bundle it up and throw it into a fire. This is consistent with the way I treat useless branches in the vineyard, the ones I've pruned because they are diseased.

But here's the trigger for me. In this story, God purposely leaves evil in the world, knowing full well that you, me, and even His Son Jesus would be born into a world of weeds. Life in the world wasn't going to be easy. In fact, it was going to be hard. Very hard. But God had ordained it this way. He said, "I created something good, something very good, but now Lucifer has infiltrated it and scattered his seed amongst my good work. We'll let the bad grow with the good. We'll let those whom I love live amongst the weeds."

Why? Why would God do that to the creation He loves?

I've found my answer in Jesus's longest sermon in Matthew 5, where He talks about salt and light:

> You are the salt of the earth. But if the salt loses its saltiness, how can it be made salty again? It is no longer good for anything, except to be thrown out and trampled underfoot.
>
> You are the light of the world. A town built on a hill cannot be hidden. Neither do people light a lamp and put it under a bowl. Instead they put it on its stand, and it gives light to everyone in the house. In the same way, let your light shine before others, that they may see your good deeds and glorify your Father in heaven. (Matthew 5:13–16)

There it is! Jesus tells us to be light to the world to glorify God. That's my purpose. That's the purpose of good fruit living amongst the weeds. Our good works don't have anything to do with earning our right to go to heaven. No, our good works show our light and demonstrates that we are good fruit, that we are children of the King. We are image-bearers of the King. We are His representatives to the weedy world. Our light and fruit demonstrate to a lost and desperate world that God is real and that His goodness will survive, thrive, and come to a full harvest. The kingdom plan of the Father will not die, be destroyed, or be quenched. It will come to be. Count on it.

Every day as I drive to work, I listen to the foghorn voice of Steve Brown on the radio. He's a wonderful teacher, very insightful. While speaking about pain and suffering in the world, I remember Steve saying that Christians aren't insulated from experiencing bad things. Just because you're a Christian doesn't mean you aren't going to get cancer or have an accident and become a paraplegic. No, as a matter of fact Steve thinks that when a non-believer gets cancer, a believing Christian gets cancer just so the world can see the difference in how Christians deal with it versus the secular world. Think about that!

There's some wisdom in this, even though we don't want it to happen to us. I certainly hope nothing like that happens to me or you for a long time, but if we don't shine, will the world ever see God? We need to trust in the provision of the Lord and walk humbly with Him. Think of how deep the Father's love, mercy, and patience is that He continues to lavish His blessings on a world of weeds.

This gives me a better understanding of God's justice. Deuteronomy 32:35 tells us that justice is the Lord's, and He will repay it. So it's not our place to dispense justice or revenge. Fruit and light do not avenge. Rather, we demonstrate, illustrate, shine, and show. Dispensing justice is for God. We are God's posterchildren and billboards to advertise to non-believers. Think of them as sleeping seeds. They have been made in the image of God and are physically alive, but their souls haven't yet been born. They haven't become spiritually alive.

You and I are beacons of hope to the sleeping seeds of this world, so that they might see in us something that makes them respond to the prompting of the Spirit calling them.

Let me unpack that a bit. Have you ever led someone to Christ? I have, but I never convinced anyone to become a believer. No, God was working on them, knocking at the door, a long time before I ever came along. I just happened to be the right billboard on the right corner of that person's life at the right time. If that person responds and accepts Christ, it's because of the work of the Father, not me.

I can win an argument and convince someone of something—I'm pretty good at this, as I've been in sales for more than thirty years—but only God changes hearts and lives. Faith in Jesus Christ is a gift from the Father. We, in our sinfulness, wouldn't participate in anything holy, because it's not in our nature. Yet if we respond to the calling of the Spirit and give our hearts to the Lord, it's only because the Father was already calling and pursuing us.

Have you ever seen a Billy Graham rally? I used to love them, because I could see the power of the Lord pulling people out of their seats to walk down to the front and claim Jesus as Lord. God bless Billy. He was a wonderful man. Did he stand up there with a lot of the flash and stirring emotional drama you see with some preachers? No. He talked Scripture and told you what it says, then invited you to come forward. It wasn't Billy... it was God! It was a powerful, inspiring sight to behold.

I have a dear friend who likes to send me video links to a young preacher who has a lot of good things to say, but he has to put on a show while saying it. This always leaves me wondering why there's such a need for hoopla and emotional manipulation. The mind that responds to such theatrics is like the seed that fell on the loose soil Jesus described. It will sprout, but because it's rooted in a cult of personality rather than the Lord, it may wither and die during a time of testing.

That's the macro view of weeds, but there is also a micro view— the weeds exist in us personally. These weeds have been growing to maturity in us our whole lives. We're born that way, full of weeds.

One Sunday, my pastor preached, "If you don't think we're born with sin, let me ask the parents here this morning, do you remember teaching your child to be selfish?" It's a great point! You don't have to teach babies to be self-centred. It's in their makeup, in their DNA.

When I became a Christ follower, many of my weeds stood out like a wolf at a rabbit convention! At my conversion, my spiritual seed became alive in me and began to emerge into a patch of already well-established weeds. The weeding needed to start. Pull 'em and burn 'em!

In other words, I had to repent. At first I thought it was me who had to get rid of the weeds and pull them out. Well, I found out I'm not very good at that. I tend to be a poor gardener when it comes to my own weeds. I leave stuff behind and generally don't get the whole root. I've discovered that my job is not to pull, but to be receptive soil and let go of the weed.

Let me explain that a bit. If you ask a gardener, "When is the best time to pick weeds?" they'll answer, "After a rain!" Why? Because the soil loosens up after the rain falls. The roots don't have as strong a grip on the soil. The soil is able to release the weed much easier than if you were trying to pull it out during a drier spell. My job is not to do the pulling as much as it is to just let go.

The Spirit is weeding. Me? My job is to be receptive, to be like clay in the hands of the potter, and to let go. I need to stop trying to tend my own garden, because I'm not very good at it. Are you still trying to tend your garden? Is it time to let go?

Harvest Time

1. Remember that phrase: "One year to seed; seven to weed." In other words, if we aren't diligent about tending unwanted seed, it will germinate and foster more unwanted stuff. Now compare this to your life—your attitudes, habits, and behaviours. What unwanted seed is being left unattended in you? Are you ready to let God weed it from you?

2. When it comes to weeding our own gardens, we aren't very thorough. We tend to skip certain weeds or not get the whole root. Are you currently striving to weed your own garden or are you ready for God to do the weeding? We have to admit our weaknesses to recognize that we need help. How are you doing in that area?

3. How are you actively shining and demonstrating Jesus in your life? Are you doing it inside the church or outside the church? Who's the last person you witnessed to and told your story? Make a list of those in your life who you want to share with, then go tell them!

Chapter Nine

Protecting the Fruit

Robins! The bane of my existence! Around the last week of July and the beginning of August, in conjunction with the glorious arrival of veraison, robins start to notice the changing colour of the berries. They get very excited indeed. I can hear them calling out in the treed bush about a hundred feet from the edge of the vineyard, triumphantly welcoming the harvest.

Here's the problem with that… their idea of ripe and my idea of ripe are two different things. They're not as picky or patient as I am in terms of waiting until the maximum amount of sugar is achieved in the berry. To a robin, a dark berry equals a good berry, period. They'll take a berry at 10 Brix or less, while I'm looking for a Brix of 22.

To prevent too much pilfering by these winged thieves, I put netting over the entire row—from the ground on one side, all the way over the top, to the ground on the other side. I secure the bottoms of the nets with firewood from my log pile, placing one log every three or four feet, on both sides. That's a lot of logs! This is how obsessive I am about protecting my harvest!

At the ends of each row, I use long wooden dowels to sew the net together so the ends aren't left open and unsecured. It takes me about twenty-four hours of solid labour to get the job done, and here's the thing… they still get in! It's like a Houdini trick. I won't be able to think of how I've left a gap anywhere, yet when I come home after work and walk the vineyard, I'll hear chirping. They scream as they fly madly into the net trying to get out. I'll chase them up and down the row until they push their way out or get tangled in the net. Then I have to release them.

Laying out the nets.

Netting in progress.

Netting complete.

It's all they do, all day long. They pop, pop, pop up and down the rows, surveying the nets, looking for a way in. They're very persistent. You'd think with the level of difficulty involved they would just move on to easier fare. But no, they love my grapes that much. The Foch berry is perfect for a bird. It's much smaller than a table grape, and very sweet.

From dawn till dusk, I worry about robins. From dusk till dawn? Raccoons.

I also use scarecrows, but birds and animals can figure out it's a fake after a while. Eventually they'll think, *Hey, that guy hasn't moved in three days! Guess the coast is clear!* And vermin aren't scared of motionless beasts, so you have to move them periodically. When I place the scarecrows in the vineyard, I talk to them like I'm leaving them there for a shift! "Okay, Joe. You just watch this area for a bit. I'll be right over there!" Pray for me, people! I need help!

Shoeless Joe reporting for duty.

Leaving Shoeless Joe for his shift in the vineyard.

I'm not the only one who's obsessed with this fight against marauding berry thieves. When Sheila and I had an opportunity to visit our friends Tom and Nicole in their homeland of Switzerland, they took us out to visit the countryside.

"There's something I think you would be interested in seeing," Tom said.

We drove to a vineyard which looked normal enough, but as we stood looking at the perfect rows, the whole vineyard sprang to life. We heard a whirring noise coming from a barn off to the side. Then we figured out that the whirring was coming from a motor that operated a pulley wheel. The pulley wheel had a length of cord that had been strategically laid through the vineyard, up and down each row, forming a continuous loop that was all connected to the one pulley. When that pulley started up, it would rotate forward for a few turns, then reverse a few turns, forward a few turns, reverse a few turns. In essence, it was pulling the cord up and down the rows two or three feet, then reverse back two or three feet.

Here's the brilliant part. Attached to the cord were flaps of foil and scary bird balloons. When this thing sparked up, the whole vineyard came alive with action. Noise! Flashing foil! Angry bird faces! It even scared me the first few times it started up.

After watching for a while, we noticed that the inventor had put the main motor on a random timer so that the length of time between runs varied. Brilliant! This was one of the most inventive ways I'd ever seen of thwarting the enemy. Others use air cannons that are motion-activated, and still others swear by human hair, bars of soap, or dead fish. Clearly, we're a group obsessed with trying to preserve our hard labour from freeloaders.

If I, as a small-time human vinekeeper, go out of my way to protect my harvest, does God also go out of His way to protect His harvest? The answer is clearly yes, because Scripture is chock full of examples of protecting angels—entire armies of angels, in fact. There are also references to God's hedge of protection.

For instance, look at Satan's complaint at the start of Job:

One day the angels came to present themselves before the Lord, and Satan also came with them. The Lord said to Satan, "Where have you come from?"

Satan answered the Lord, "From roaming throughout the earth, going back and forth on it."

Then the Lord said to Satan, "Have you considered my servant Job? There is no one on earth like him; he is blameless and upright, a man who fears God and shuns evil."

"Does Job fear God for nothing?" Satan replied. "Have you not put a hedge around him and his household and everything he has? You have blessed the work of his hands, so that his flocks and herds are spread throughout the land. But now stretch out your hand and strike everything he has, and he will surely curse you to your face."

The Lord said to Satan, "Very well, then, everything he has is in your power, but on the man himself do not lay a finger."

Then Satan went out from the presence of the Lord. (Job 1:6–12)

Satan essentially said, "Of course Job loves you! You've protected him. But allow him to lose everything and he'll turn on you."

Surprisingly, God then allows Satan to have his way, except he cannot hurt Job himself.

"God, why would you hurt Job in this way?" the reader might ask. Indeed, Job asked the same question, arguing that he had done nothing to deserve it. He wanted some answers from God. Well, God showed up, big-time! He said to Job, *"Brace yourself like a man; I will question you, and you shall answer me"* (Job 38:3).

For the next four chapters, God reminded Job that He is God and that His ways, mind, knowledge, and power are well beyond Job's ability to comprehend. Job wasn't in a position to question God's purposes and motives.

Thousands of years later, I'm no different from Job. I don't understand, and sometimes I forget and question God as to His timing and motives.

On August 5, 2009 at 6:05 p.m., I lay in my kitchen dying.

Have I got your attention?

I came home that evening after a day at the office to do some work in the vineyard. I was going to plant some new rows, and in preparation I had sprayed them with Roundup weeks earlier to kill the vegetation. My goal that day was to go out into the vineyard with my shovel and turn the soil, priming them for receiving new vines next year.

The area where I was working was approximately three hundred feet from the house. I mindlessly stuck the shovel in the ground three times, then started to feel millions of pinpricks on my legs. It took me a second or two to realize what was happening. As I looked down, I saw yellow jacket wasps all over my legs! Then I realized I was also getting stung on my arms, face, and back. I swatted and backpedalled as fast as I could. If someone had been watching, I probably would have looked like an insane German slap dancer!

I danced my way backwards until the stinging and biting stopped.[17] Then I saw what was going on: clouds of wasps were flying to the area where I had just been working. I had accidentally unearthed a yellow jacket colony.

As I came to find out later, yellow jackets come in different types. Some build nests aboveground in trees or under eavestroughs. Then there are those that build nests in the ground. It had been so well hidden that I hadn't been able to see it.

I stood there for a second, stunned. Then I thought, *I need to get my shovel!* It was still stuck in the ground, right where I had left it. So I turned and started walking to the house to get my can of wasp spray. I was bound and determined to get my shovel back!

At this point, I wasn't concerned about being stung because I had been stung before and nothing more than a red welt had shown up. I had seen other people's stings swell up like a catcher's mitt, but that had never happened to me.

I walked the three hundred feet back to the house, got my can of spray, and trudged back to the scene of the crime. By this time,

---

[17] I learned afterwards that wasps can bite and sting at the same time. A double threat!

the wasps were abuzz around the nest entrance, and now I could clearly see what looked like a mouse hole going underground. That was my target! I aimed and fired that can of spray, putting down a suppressing layer of foam around the area.

Instantly, the soldiers started coming at me again. I then rushed the hole, stuck the nozzle in, and gave it a huge blast. Wasps aren't as smart as, say, a chipmunk and they don't have a second escape hole. They have one way in, and one way out. Hasta la vista, baby!

I grabbed my shovel, thinking I couldn't keep working in this area. I decided to go a little further up the row to continue my work.

As I started to walk up the row, it started to hit me. It felt like someone had their finger on the dimmer switch of my life and was starting to turn it down.

Hmmmm, maybe I need to go to the house and sit down for a bit. With every step I took, my legs got heavier and heavier. *This is getting pretty bad pretty quick...*

I was now a few steps from the garage, still about a hundred feet from the house. I didn't know if I was going to make it!

I pushed myself to get to the kitchen door, and by this point I knew I was in crisis. I needed to get to the phone to call 911. I put my hand on the door and remember begging God and thinking of Sheila.

Not today, Lord! Please not today!

I got into the house and got to the phone. By now, my hands were shaking and my eyesight had started to blur. I focused as hard as I could and pressed 9-1-1.

The voice came on line: "This is 911. Do you want ambulance or police?"

"Ambulance."

"What's the nature of the problem?"

"I've been stung by wasps."

"Are you at..." She read out my address to me.

"Yes."

And with that, it was as if someone flicked a light switch. Everything went black.

I learned a lot afterwards about what happened next, but at that point I was just lying on the kitchen floor. I'd smacked the back of my head on the kitchen counter when I passed out.

The ambulance got there in approximately ten minutes. They must have been flying! I do remember seeing some flashes of light before my eyes and hearing a voice say, "Stay with us, Todd!"

As I lay in the darkness of my mind, I think I figured out that I was at the hospital, and still alive. I looked to my left and saw a clock on the wall. It was 7:30 p.m. An hour and a half had gone missing from my life.

I then had a bizarre thought. Natasha, a woman who went to our church, worked at the hospital as a nurse, and I wondered if she was working. Why would I think that? I don't know, but I turned my head to the right, and who was standing right there looking at me? Natasha!

I mustered the strength to say, "Natasha, call Sheila and let her know I'm okay."

Then I passed out again.

I didn't really know if I was going to be okay, but at least I was alive.

A little while later, I looked up and saw that it was 9:30 p.m., and Sheila was standing beside my bed.

She's so beautiful! I thought.

Sheila started to share her story about coming home after work and finding the garage and house doors open. She worked as a librarian at the local library, and in the warmth of summer she rode her bike to work. As she'd rode up the laneway that day, she hadn't had any sense that there was something wrong. Seeing the doors open like that could have been normal, so she didn't think anything of it at first.

She'd gone into the house and called for me. No answer. Then she'd gone back outside and called for me. No answer. She'd then returned to the house and saw that something had happened in the kitchen. The kitchen mats had been pushed back up against the walls and flipped over. The wireless phone was on the ground. Muddy footprints were on the floor.

She panicked, immediately jumping to the conclusion that I'd had a fight with an intruder and had been taken.[18] She was about to call 911 when she heard a small voice in her head: "Go upstairs and check the answering machine."

She went upstairs to the office, opened the door, and saw a blinking red light on the machine. She hit the play button and heard the message from Natasha telling her that I was at the hospital, and that I was okay.

By the next morning, a Friday, the attending emergency physician came to my bed at 4:30 and said, "Todd, we're going to be moving you to the cardiac ward. You've had a heart attack."

What!? I was stunned.

"Was it the wasps?" I asked.

"Yes, it was the wasps. When the ambulance attendants found you, your blood pressure was down to sixty. They hit you with two EpiPens. Now your bloodwork tells us you have an enzyme in your blood that only shows up if you've had a heart attack."

"Well, how bad is it?" I asked. "I don't feel that bad."

"We can't tell until we do some more tests."

They moved me up to the cardiac ward, where I got the best care I could imagine. When they told me they were coming by to get blood every twenty minutes, they meant it. I wasn't getting out of there until the enzyme level started coming down. They also wanted to perform an echocardiogram on my heart. They did this, and by Saturday morning I was ready to go home.

Within a month of the event, I underwent a full stress test on my heart—nuclear isotope injection, treadmill, and scanner—and everything checked out okay.

In the months afterward, I was referred to an allergy specialist because there was concern that I was anaphylactic, meaning that I could get a major reaction and die if I got stung again. I started an immunotherapy program to build up an immunity to yellow jackets. I was tested for all varieties of stinging insects and fire ants.

The doctor who looked at my skin tests—they inject a trace amount under the skin, and if you're allergic you have a massive

18 She reads a lot of murder mysteries!

reaction—said, "You don't show signs of being allergic to anything. Sure, the yellow jacket injection is a little more red than the others, but if you were allergic I would have expected to see a more pronounced reaction. Having said that, it would be irresponsible of me not to recommend you for immunotherapy treatment."

So I started the treatments. I went every week and they injected me with ever-increasing amounts of actual yellow jacket venom. I got three injections per session, then sat for twenty minutes between injections. We weren't supposed to move on to the next level of strength if we had a skin reaction larger than a quarter. I went week after week and had no reactions, at least not on the surface.

On the last week, I went in for my "graduation shot." After that, I would only need to go back once per month instead of every week.

I got my graduation shot on a Tuesday, and on Thursday morning I was back out in the vineyard with a cup of coffee, walking the rows. I bent over to lift a branch that had fallen to the ground and needed tying. When I leaned forward, I felt like my head was going to explode!

I walked back into the house and said to Sheila, "I don't feel so good."

"Your face is purple!"

I lifted up my shirt and I saw that my stomach was blotchy red, and my face was indeed graduating to a nice shade of purple. My blood pressure was sky high.

We went to the emergency room and I told them my story of woe.

"Well, clearly you are having a reaction to that treatment," the nurse told me.

No kidding! As I lay in my bed, the doctor came in with an IV which had a cocktail of Benadryl, Reactine, and some other substance to deal with the reaction. Sheila watched as they set up the IV. She said it was amazing to watch, and that as soon as the liquid entered my body my colour went back to normal. It was like shaking an Etch-a-sketch and clearing the screen!

The doctor came in and told me I would feel okay for a while, but that the reaction would come back. I would probably have intermittent attacks for the next year.

That's exactly what happened. While sitting in church, I'd feel the tips of my ears getting hot. I'd lean over to Sheila and say, "Here we go." Sure enough, my face would start to go red and I would need to take some medication to counteract the attack.

It was a trying time in my life, to say the least.

The original allergist I saw was a little panicked. I went back to see him and he was anxious for me to sign a waiver, which I did. He ordered a bunch of tests to see what was going on. I later asked my family doctor what these tests were. He looked at the list and said, "Boy, this guy is grasping at straws!" It turns out the allergist was ordering tests for all sorts of rare cancers.

In the end, my doctor gave me some Prednisone which knocked the reactions right out.[19]

Soon after my run-in with the wasps, while I was still in the hospital, a well-meaning Christian couple came to visit. The wife said to me, "What do you think God is trying to teach you through this?"

Boy did I struggle with that. Essentially she was saying that God had orchestrated the wasp attack to teach me some kind of lesson. I don't think God operates that way.

I shared this with my pastor at the time and told him that I really didn't think God had been trying to grab my attention and teach me some sort of life lesson. He very wisely pointed me in the direction of Philippians 2:25–27, which says,

> But I think it is necessary to send back to you Epaphroditus, my brother, co-worker and fellow soldier, who is also your messenger, whom you sent to take care of my needs. For he longs for all of you and is distressed because you heard he was ill. Indeed he was ill, and almost died. But God had mercy on him, and not on him only but also on me, to spare me sorrow upon sorrow. (Philippians 2:25–27)

---

[19] Now, I know some medical professionals may be reading this, and opinions will be flying. Just know that I'm not sharing this to question the quality of aftercare I received. My point is to talk about how God protected me throughout my trial.

Paul was writing to the Philippians and introducing us to Epaphroditus, who Paul identified as a brother, co-worker, and fellow soldier in Christ. Paul wrote that Epaphroditus was very ill, even to the point of death, but God had mercy on both Epaphroditus and Paul to save Paul from *"sorrow upon sorrow."*

Had God been trying to teach Epaphroditus a lesson through the illness or had God merely been there through the man's rescue and healing? Had God been trying to teach me a lesson through the wasps or had He merely been with me through my rescue and healing? Had God been saving Sheila sorrow upon sorrow?

We live in a messed-up world, an imperfect vineyard, and sometimes accidents happen. I don't think God plans cuts, scrapes, skinned knees, and bumps on the head as a way of instructing us. However, God does step into those situations to protect and provide for us. The church rallies around families dealing with cancer, offering meals, support, and prayer. That is God in action.

In my case, had there been an angel pushing me toward the phone so I wouldn't die that day? Maybe. Had God been intervening when Natasha showed up to be my messenger to Sheila? What about the small voice that had instructed Sheila to check the answering machine?

All I know is that when I read the Bible from cover to cover, I encounter a God who loves us intensely, a God who loves us so much that He had a plan from the beginning of time to save us by sacrificing Himself. Through this plan, He had skin in the game. He came down to the earth and walked as we walk. He bled as we bleed. I'm sure He got cold, fell ill, blew his nose, and passed gas just like the rest of us.

But in the end, He did something you or I could never do—He lived a perfect life and took on the sins of the world. That's how much He loves you. That's how far He's willing to go to protect you. You are the fruit of His vineyard.

He paid your price. He ransomed you. He set you free. We bear good fruit if we're part of the vine, and we bear this fruit not as a repayment; nothing we do could ever repay Him. We bear good fruit out of love for the one who loved us first.

He loved you before you knew Him. He loved you before you were even friends. God spanned time and space to deliver you from your mess, to create a way for you to be with Him for eternity. That's a good God. He provides grace—unmerited favour, meaning you can't earn it. No other religion in the world talks of grace. Grace is our safety net. The wonderful majesty of grace finds a sinner like me, washes me clean, erases my sin, and breaks my chains and bonds so I can willingly put on His yoke. It's light and easy. Jesus said,

Take my yoke upon you and learn from me, for I am gentle and humble in heart, and you will find rest for your souls. For my yoke is easy and my burden is light." (Matthew 11:29–30)

I put on that yoke to pull and work in the fields, to bear fruit for my King. I don't do it to earn a wage, but because I want to please Him.

When I read stories like the one in Job, I have to take the fuller picture of God into account. If you look at that story in isolation, it looks like God is the orchestrator of Job's demise. Satan says to God, "Job loves you because you keep him like a pet and protect him. But stretch out your hand against him, and he will surely curse you." Satan is essentially suggesting that God is the author of the destruction. In other words, Satan is saying, "You're the shooter, God, and I'm the gun. Any harm that comes to Job is on you."

If we only read that part of the story, we could come to the wrong conclusion. But when we read the full counsel of Scripture, we see that God isn't like that. He's loving, patient, merciful, and longsuffering. The Father has been calling to His wayward sons and daughters, waiting for them to come home.

Satan is the liar and the deceiver. Even in this exchange, he's lying to God and twisting the truth. Satan is the one who wants to hurt Job.

Another exchange in Scripture helps me understand this. In Luke, Jesus had broken the bread and given the cup in their communion together. He had again predicted His death. Then he and Peter had this exchange:

"Simon, Simon, Satan has asked to sift all of you as wheat. But I have prayed for you, Simon, that your faith may not fail. And when you have turned back, strengthen your brothers."
But [Peter] replied, "Lord, I am ready to go with you to prison and to death."
Jesus answered, "I tell you, Peter, before the rooster crows today, you will deny three times that you know me." (Luke 11:31–34)

Jesus called Peter by his old name, Simon. This was the name he'd gone by before meeting Christ. Why? Probably because Peter was acting in his old Simon mode, operating under his own strength and knowledge versus his new self.

Jesus said to Peter, "Satan has asked to sift all of you as wheat." Similar to the Job exchange, Satan had been asking God to hurt Peter and test him, to break him and turn him from God. Then Jesus added, "But I have prayed for you."

Jesus is our protector. Jesus is the safety net of our lives.

Peter was a man of extremes, so he replied, "Lord, I am ready to go with you to prison and to death."

And yet before the rooster crowed, Peter was going to deny Jesus three times. Upon hearing the rooster crow after he had cursed and sworn he didn't know Jesus, Peter and Jesus locked eyes. Peter wept bitterly, knowing that God had seen the failure of his character.

But the story doesn't end here. Later, after the resurrection, Peter was out fishing when he had this beautiful exchange with the risen Christ:

Afterward Jesus appeared again to his disciples, by the Sea of Galilee. It happened this way: Simon Peter, Thomas (also known as Didymus), Nathanael from Cana in Galilee, the sons of Zebedee, and two other disciples were together. "I'm going out to fish," Simon Peter told them, and they said, "We'll go with you." So they went out and got into the boat, but that night they caught nothing.

Early in the morning, Jesus stood on the shore, but the disciples did not realize that it was Jesus.

He called out to them, "Friends, haven't you any fish?"

"No," they answered.

He said, "Throw your net on the right side of the boat and you will find some." When they did, they were unable to haul the net in because of the large number of fish.

Then the disciple whom Jesus loved said to Peter, "It is the Lord!" As soon as Simon Peter heard him say, "It is the Lord," he wrapped his outer garment around him (for he had taken it off) and jumped into the water. The other disciples followed in the boat, towing the net full of fish, for they were not far from shore, about a hundred yards. When they landed, they saw a fire of burning coals there with fish on it, and some bread.

Jesus said to them, "Bring some of the fish you have just caught." So Simon Peter climbed back into the boat and dragged the net ashore. It was full of large fish, 153, but even with so many the net was not torn. Jesus said to them, "Come and have breakfast." None of the disciples dared ask him, "Who are you?" They knew it was the Lord. Jesus came, took the bread and gave it to them, and did the same with the fish. This was now the third time Jesus appeared to his disciples after he was raised from the dead.

When they had finished eating, Jesus said to Simon Peter, "Simon son of John, do you love me more than these?"

"Yes, Lord," he said, "you know that I love you."

Jesus said, "Feed my lambs."

Again Jesus said, "Simon son of John, do you love me?"

He answered, "Yes, Lord, you know that I love you."

Jesus said, "Take care of my sheep."

The third time he said to him, "Simon son of John, do you love me?"

Peter was hurt because Jesus asked him the third time, "Do you love me?" He said, "Lord, you know all things; you know that I love you."

Jesus said, "Feed my sheep. Very truly I tell you, when you were younger you dressed yourself and went where you wanted; but when you are old you will stretch out your hands, and someone else will dress you and lead you where you do not want to go." Jesus said this to indicate the kind of death by which Peter would glorify God. Then he said to him, "Follow me!" (John 21:1–19)

Isn't that beautiful!? The resurrected Jesus stopped by to cook His disciples some breakfast after supplying a net full of fish. He pulled Peter aside and lovingly forgave him for the earlier denials. He then instructed Peter to take care of His sheep. In other words, "Take care of my church."

Jesus had a plan and crafted goodness out of ashes.

It's worth noting here that Jesus was also telling Peter how his life was going to end. As believers, we today are no different than Peter, and no better than our Master who suffered tremendously and was despised, beaten, spit on, and scorned. That's why, after His last lesson on the vines and branches, Jesus said to His disciples:

If the world hates you, keep in mind that it hated me first. If you belonged to the world, it would love you as its own. As it is, you do not belong to the world, but I have chosen you out of the world. That is why the world hates you. Remember what I told you: "A servant is not greater than his master." If they persecuted me, they will persecute you also. If they obeyed my teaching, they will obey yours also. They will treat you this way because of my name, for they do not know the one who sent me. If I had not come and spoken to them, they would not be guilty of sin; but now they have no excuse for their sin. Whoever hates me hates my Father as well. If I had not done among them the works no one else did, they would not be guilty of sin. As it is, they have seen, and yet they have hated both me and my Father. But this is to fulfill what is written in their Law: "They hated me without reason." (John 15:18–25)

It's not going to be an easy ride, my friends, but we can know in the end that there is a Master Gardener who loves us, has a plan for us, and will see it through to completion. Whatever your set of circumstances, whatever your situation, have confidence that you are loved more than you could ever understand. God will bring beauty out of ashes.

Harvest Time

1. I shared my story about the wasps and suggested how God showed up in the process. Describe a time when God provided for you. What did it look like? How was it done?

2. We looked at the example of Job and contrasted it with Jesus's dealing with Peter. Do these exchanges give you a new perspective to help understand the pain in your life? What comfort can you draw about God or Christ from this discussion?

3. In Luke 14:28–35, Jesus talks about counting the cost of being a disciple and following Him. This chapter then ends by examining John 15:18–25, where Jesus tells us that our lives aren't going to be easy. How have you experienced persecution or paid a cost for your faith? How has this changed you? Was it worth it?

Chapter Ten
The Harvest

It has now been a full season, and the fruit is ripening on the vine. It's probably the last week of September. I take a selection of random berries from different areas of the vineyard and put them in a Ziplock bag. I mush them around to create juice, and then I drop a bit of that nectar onto my Brix refractor and look through it, into the light. It's time for the harvest!

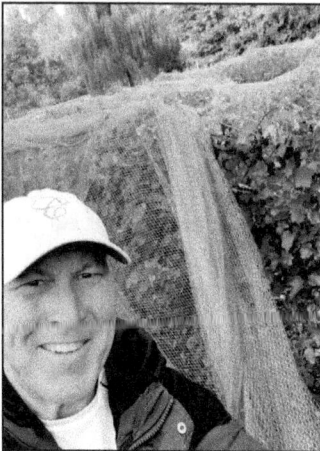

Harvest time!
The nets are coming off!

Harvest humour.
Thanks, Betsy!

This is a big day! I prep all my bins and put the call out to my able-bodied workers. My wonderful in-laws come in from Elmira to pick for the day.[20]

The day starts with peeling back the nets and revealing the glorious fruit on the vines. The air is filled with the aroma of sweet grapes. I try to get an early start, when the temperatures are cooler, because there will be less wasp activity and any wasps that are out will be sluggish due to the cold. As the day heats up, however, the wasp and bee activity becomes intense, for they can sense the season is nearing its end. They're frantic to get their last nutrition of the year before they die.

The wasps' goal for the year has been to service the queen, and the queen will be the only one to survive the winter. The rest of her colony dies off as she hibernates, usually huddled up in my woodpile under a flap of bark. I might meet her at some point when I bring in a piece of wood to burn in the fireplace and she emerges to start flying around the room. This will cause a lot of excitement with rolled-up newspapers!

The harvest work goes quickly! We snip the ripe clusters from the branches and place them in the bin. We don't drop them; we place them. And we bob and weave like prize fighters, looking down low on the branches and then working our way up, seeking out fruit that may be hidden by a leaf. And all the while, we're dodging wasps.

Oh, and did I mention the ladybug lookalikes? The Asian beetles like to get in there too, and they get their heads buried into a berry, dining on the juicy fruit. We try to flick them out as best we can, because even one in a batch of wine can taint the taste. Perhaps you've killed one in your house and smelled the acrid stench they give off. Imagine that in your wine!

It usually takes four or five hours to take in the full harvest of Foch. The white variety, Seyval Blanc, gets harvested three or four weeks later, and I usually do that myself because there are only fifty vines.

---

[20] Elmira is known for its Mennonite population, and in the Niagara region many of the workers are migrant pickers, so I call my in-laws my Mexican Mennonites. Perhaps that's a little politically incorrect, but we get a chuckle out of it anyhow.

Once done, we will have taken in approximately four hundred fifty pounds of fruit at a Brix of about 22. This will make approximately one hundred sixty bottles of wine.

Bin full of grapes.

I then take the bins over to Klaus's place where they're immediately put through a destemming/crushing machine to prep them for pressing. Klaus will let the fruit "sit on the skins" for about a week before pressing. This means that you don't press the juice out of the berry right away, but allow the mixture of juice and skins to marinate and sit in a bin for a period of time. By letting the mixture sit after crushing, all the flavours and tannins of the skin are allowed to be released into the juice.

Once pressed, the long wait begins. Klaus will be busy making the wine, and I'll wait until the process brings forth a wonderful celebration of complex smells, aromas, tastes, and sensations. As of the writing of this book, I'm still waiting for my 2016 Foch, which has been maturing for about a year and a half in an oak barrel. We have high expectations for it because it was one of our driest years and we got one of our highest Brix numbers—22.2. I hope to be raising a glass soon.

Foch in the press.

It has been my hope and prayer that as this book goes along you have gained a minor insight into the activity of keeping grape vines. But more importantly, I hope you can see how Jesus's final lesson becomes more vibrant by learning more about the vineyard. Even if you didn't gain new insight, I think it's important to be reminded again and again about who God is, how He works, what He is trying to accomplish, and what we as His followers are supposed to do.

I also hope that this method of looking into the character and activity of God through the work of the vineyard has inspired you to take a keener interest in how the Creator of all things reveals Himself through His creation. Whatever your task, whatever your work, I'm sure the fingerprints and signature of the Master Gardener are clearly visible, if only you look for them.

As we close off our harvest, I want to go back to Jesus's final lesson:

I am the true vine, and my Father is the gardener. He cuts off every branch in me that bears no fruit, while every branch that does bear fruit he prunes so that it will be even more fruitful. You are already clean because of the word I have spoken to you. Remain in me, as I also remain in you. No branch can bear fruit by itself; it must remain in the vine. Neither can you bear fruit unless you remain in me.

I am the vine; you are the branches. If you remain in me and I in you, you will bear much fruit; apart from me you can do nothing. If you do not remain in me, you are like a branch that is thrown away and withers; such branches are picked up, thrown into the fire and burned. If you remain in me and my words remain in you, ask whatever you wish, and it will be done for you. This is to my Father's glory, that you bear much fruit, showing yourselves to be my disciples.

As the Father has loved me, so have I loved you. Now remain in my love. If you keep my commands, you will remain in my love, just as I have kept my Father's commands and remain in his love. I have told you this so that my joy may be in you and that your joy may be complete. My command is this: Love each other as I have loved you. Greater love has no one than this: to lay down one's life for one's friends. You are my friends if you do what I command. I no longer call you servants, because a servant does not know his master's business. Instead, I have called you friends, for everything that I learned from my Father I have made known to you. You did not choose me, but I chose you and appointed you so that you might go and bear fruit—fruit that will last—and so that whatever you ask in my name the Father will give you. This is my command: Love each other. (John 15:1–17)

Jesus is the vine, and we are the branches. I am not the source. I am not the vine. I am not the one in charge. Because apart from the vine, I can do nothing—at least nothing of value.

Do you want to live for value? Do you want your life to have purpose? Are you going to shine as a light for the Kingdom of God, or will you hoard your light under a bowl, keeping it to yourself? I hope you choose to shine!

It is to the Father's glory that we shine and bear much fruit! The fruit we bear brings joy to the Father, but more importantly it shows a dark and desperate world that God is very much alive and well! He's still in the redemption business. He cares for and loves you intensely, and He's calling you to actually be part of the work He's doing. How cool is that?

I may not be Billy Graham or Mother Teresa, leading thousands and thousands to Christ, but in my neck of the vineyard I can serve a meal, encourage a friend, show kindness to a stranger, and suffer abuse for being known as a Christian. I can bear the best fruit I can to glorify my King. Would you join me in that?

I am to remain in His love, remain connected to Christ, remain connected to the vine.

Now we have a job to do! Scripture tells us about grace and says there's nothing we can do to earn our salvation. True enough. But there is something I can do to stay rooted to the vine, and to show myself to be a Christ follower: I remain in His love by keeping His commands. This is a call for an active response. I'm being called to do something, not to earn something, but to demonstrate that I'm on Team Jesus.

If you think about clubs and associations, cults and religions, what they want is for people to demonstrate that they are part of the team. Many of them want money. Some want a secret handshake. Others want a certain kind of dress or uniform. Still others want their people to perform tasks, duties, and rituals.

What does Jesus want? He said, *"Love each other as I have loved you"* (John 15:12).

There it is. That's the membership fee, the task, the goal: love each other as Jesus has loved you.

Remember who you were before knowing Christ. Remember how you used to behave. Remember what you said out loud and what you thought in private. Dwell on that for a minute and know that Jesus loved you enough to come to earth, walk where you walk, take your abuse, carry a cross, willingly go to a hill, take three spikes in your place, and die your death—all because He loves you and wants to be with you.

Your repayment is to love others that much.

Jesus doesn't stop there. He says that we are His friends! If you don't get goosebumps running up the back of your spine when you read that, we need to check you for a heartbeat. I think this is one of the greatest, guard-dropping, pride-crushing statements in the Bible: *"Greater love has no one than this: to lay down one's life for one's friends. You are my friends if you do what I command"* (John 15:13–14).

He laid down His life for me. Have you laid down your life for someone?

This lesson has made me a better husband than I ever thought I could be. Don't get me wrong—I'm not perfect and never will be—but understanding the depth of Christ's love has shown me how to lay down my life for Sheila. I love her so intensely.

It wasn't always that way. In the early days of our marriage, it was still a lot about me. That's how I thought for the first twenty-four years of my life. I filtered everything in my life through this question: how will this affect Todd? I was very selfish, very self-centred.

After I responded to the calling of Christ? Different story. I wanted to do things for her. I wanted to please her, because I had a much deeper understanding of how much I had been forgiven by Jesus, and how much Jesus loved me.

As my understanding of Jesus's love began to manifest in my life, I changed my filter to a new question: how will this please God? I began to have a servant's heart when it came to my wife. Instead of wanting things out of our relationship, I wanted to invest into the relationship—to build and grow and improve.

And here comes the kicker, folks. As I changed my filter and focus, as I started to invest in my marriage, Sheila began to see the change, and she too began investing.[21] I would do something for her, and she would see my love and want to do something for me. Then I would see her love and want to do even more for her. We entered a really sweet dance.

I know some of you aren't impressed by this romantic banter, but this also affects how we operate in the unbelieving world. If you haven't done so already, find a charity, find a cause—outside of

---

[21] It's not like she hadn't been investing in the relationship before, only now she invested more.

taking care of yourself and your family—and serve. Give, people, give! Lay down your life for the one who loved you first. Love each other as Christ has loved you.

Sheila and I founded Rising Angels, along with Katarina, to be God's hands and feet, to be a physical ambassador of hope to victims entrapped in prostitution. This has been nothing short of an honour and a privilege. We've been called to carry an unpopular message to a desensitized world: prostitution is paid rape, not a financial transaction between two consenting adults. Prostitution is human trafficking, period.

We have found our cause to bear fruit. Have you found yours? What concerns you? What upsets you? Find that cause and show the love of Christ.

At Rising Angels, we provide a parent support group. When your baby girl is lured into prostitution by a smooth-talking pimp and then entrapped through threats of violence or the release of a sex tape, you're thrown into a vortex of pain and confusion. There are thousands of exploited persons in the Greater Toronto Area, and the vast majority of them want out. That's just Toronto. Prostitution and human trafficking are everywhere. It's a sickness that lives closer to home than you realize—closer than you probably even want to know.[22]

Jesus tells us that we now have access to know His business. He has made known to us everything He has learned from His Father: *"I no longer call you servants, because a servant does not know his master's business. Instead, I have called you friends, for everything that I learned from my Father I have made known to you"* (John 15:15). How cool is that?

I've worked in the corporate world for thirty-five years, and I can tell you that one of the gripes most employees have is not being told the clear plans and direction of the company. Can I get an amen? If you've worked in the corporate world, I'm sure you know what I'm talking about. But here Jesus says, "I've let you inside the boardroom. I'm letting you see the plan, because you are my friends." The business

---

[22] If any of what I'm writing stirs your heart, reach out to us at www.risingangels.net. We need your help and support.

plan for Jesus Inc. can be found inside the pages of the Holy Bible. Crack it open and read the prospectus! If you want to know what the game plan is for this corporation, read the Bible and get familiar with what it says.

I'm a small-time investor and I try to be a good steward of the resources God gives me. I buy equity in solid companies—most of the time. I've had some lemons and I've had some wins, but here is my confession: when these companies send me annual reports, I don't read them. I know I should, to be informed, but I rationalize my laziness by saying something to myself like this: "I only have a hundred shares. My vote doesn't count." So I put it in the recycling bin.

But Jesus is telling us, "I made you a full partner! You are a major stakeholder here!" He's still the CEO, but we have a big part to play. We need to read the annual report and understand what Jesus learned from the Father.

Here are our final instructions before game time:

You did not choose me, but I chose you and appointed you so that you might go and bear fruit—fruit that will last—and so that whatever you ask in my name the Father will give you. This is my command: Love each other. (John 15:16–17)

Yes, Jesus was talking to His chosen twelve, but He is also talking to us. He chose you! He chose me! Before the foundation of the earth, before the beginning of time, the ever-present God saw the whole story in real time and knew you were going to give your heart to Him. It's true. And you have been appointed to go and bear fruit.

You haven't been appointed to stay in a neat, clean Christian bubble. The Pharisees tried that with Judaic law and Jesus didn't seem to be impressed. Jesus is asking you to become active fruit growers, and you are to bear much fruit that will last. Kingdom fruit—and kingdom fruit comes through loving each other. Love each other!

Maybe we all need to wear that on a T-shirt, or on post-it notes, or as reminders on our phones... whatever it takes. Can you imagine the change that would happen in this world if we thought this before we acted, or reacted? Trust me, I'm still learning. I still have moments of huge, guilt-wrenching failure, but we need to try to do this a little more, and do it a little better, each day.

Thank you so much for spending this time with me. If not in this life, maybe the next, we can celebrate the Lord together. God bless. Now go bear fruit! Put down the book and *go!*

> *"For my thoughts are not your thoughts, neither are your ways my ways,"* declares the Lord. *"As the heavens are higher than the earth, so are my ways higher than your ways and my thoughts than your thoughts."* (Isaiah 55:8–9)

Harvest Time

1. Remember what you did and what you thought before you knew Christ—maybe even what you thought about Christians. How has your love grown? How have you changed? What would help you go deeper?
2. As best as you can, describe what it means to you to be a friend of the King. How is the filter and focus of your life changing? Is your life still about the things immediately around you or is it about growing on a larger scale?
3. You haven't been called to remain in a clean Christian bubble. What are you doing to get your hands dirty for Christ? What is your thirty, sixty, or ninety-day plan to get busy for the kingdom? Go make a difference!

Conclusion

I'd like to share a beautiful prayer I received from a good friend of mine, Mark. He spoke it one morning at church, and while I was listening to it I thought of you reading this book. I think you need to hear it, too. Let these words minister to your souls.

Lord God, You are worthy of all our praise, all the glory we can give You. You are holy, You are our strength, You are our comfort, You are our rock, our stronghold, our defender, our protector, our deliverer. Thank You.

God, You so loved the world that You gave Your one and only Son that whosoever believes in Him shall not perish but have eternal life. For You did not send Your Son into the world to condemn the world, but to save the world through Him.

Thank You. Help us to accept Your gift.

We want to live in Your kingdom. We want to see Your will done here on the earth as it is in heaven. You have overcome this world and You have already won. The victory is Yours.

You pursue us, You show us the way, and You offer us Your mercy. Help us to keep our hearts soft and our knees flexible, ready to kneel at Your feet.

In our acts of worship to You, allow us to offer our bodies as living sacrifices. Help us to keep them holy and pleasing to You. Lead us to be transformed by the renewing of our minds.

Give us the courage to honestly surrender ourselves so we can be filled with the forgiveness, grace, and peace You offer us. With no excuses or justification, let us swallow our pride, face our mistakes, own our issues, and confess the guilt of our sins to You, admitting that we need forgiveness and recognizing that we cannot pay for it ourselves.

You died for each one of us—not just the person beside me, but me. You died for me! Help us to move forward accepting Your forgiveness for ourselves! We can stop thinking we have to pay for it and actually let Jesus die for us!

As this truth from the Holy Spirit is revealed to us, and as it takes shape in our minds and hearts, we pray that our strength will also be renewed so that we can face temptations. Free us from a life of serving two masters.

You have called and equipped each one of us. You want Your name lifted up through each one of us. Help us live that out right where we are. Help us to allow Christ to set the direction for our lives.

www.ingramcontent.com/pod-product-compliance
Lightning Source LLC
LaVergne TN
LVHW021346080426
835508LV00020B/2146